Meal Prep

For Weight Loss, Vibrant Skin And Heathy Hair

By
Gareth Jaiden

DISCLAIMER

The information presented in this book solely and fully represents the views of the author as of the date of publication. Any omission, or potential misrepresentation of, an peoples or companies is entirely unintentional. As a result of changing information, conditions or contexts, this author reserves the right to alter content at their sole discretion impunity.

The report is for informational purposes only and while every attempt has been made to verify the information contained herein, the author assumes no responsibility for errors, inaccuracies, and omissions. Each person has unique needs and this book cannot take these individual differences into account. For ease of use, all links in this report are redirected through this link to facilitate an future changes and minimize dead links.

TABLE OF CONTENTS

INTRODUCTION TO MEAL PREPPING

What Is Meal Prepping?

Meal preparation essentially means that you plan ahead of time what you are going to eat for that day, week, or even month. By having a definitive plan what will be on the menu for breakfast, lunch, and dinner, you help prevent yourself from ever having to drive to get fast food, or order pizza to eat at home.

Better yet, by having meals ready to cook, or leftovers that can be used the following day (s), you have complete control over everything that is set on your kitchen table.

When focus is placed on your daily nutrition, not only will you be able to improve your health but also lose weight since you will be eating in a more nutritious manner. When this is priority number one, healthier habits will develop, and you will find your life turning around and becoming much more confident. This is also the perfect way to re-focus yourself on a health commitment that may have gone astray over the past year or two.

First off, it's important to plan what meals you are going to cook. It will really help if you start out with a small time-frame for two or three days, no more than a week at first. Don't over-complicate things trying to prepare the most elaborate, fanciest meals around.

Keep it straightforward and healthy, that's the primary concern here. Once you have your plan in hand, you can then make your grocery list, so you will have everything needed to prepare all those meals.

Cooking extra portions is one of the best tips you should get in the habit of doing when it comes to meal prepping. For instance, if you are planning to cook whole wheat pasta with turkey meatballs and a salad for dinner, simply cook a couple of extra portions and you will then have perfect travel sized meals for lunch the following day. If you don't feel like having the same meal two days in a row, you can always freeze the meal and enjoy later on in the week.

Having snacks already portioned and stored will increase the likelihood your family members remain eating healthy.

Your freezer is your friend, so get in the habit of storing meals that are already appropriately portion sized into containers and label with the date, so you know when it was prepared. You can do the same thing with snacks too. When you purchase fruit and veggies from the market, cut them into snack-sized bites and portion into baggies or containers. Label and place in the freezer if you aren't planning on eating them in the next few days.

You will find that when you plan out your meals for the upcoming days/week in mind, you will lessen the trips to fast food spots, and at the same time keep everyone eating in a more healthy manner. Here's the perfect opportunity to start developing a healthy eating plan to keep you focused on nutrition and appropriate portion sizes which in turn will lead to weight loss and a stronger commitment to maintaining a healthy life.

Why The Meal Prep Is Important

Have you ever considered meal prep and planning?

Don't think it applies to you? Wondering why you should bother? What's in it for you?

Meal prep is often considered something you do when you want to lose weight, or save time. But there are reasons why everyone should do this more often. Here are some extra tips on why everyone should consider doing it, at least some of the time:

❖ You Save Money

One of the top reasons to start meal prepping is that you will save money. That's because you're able to buy more foods in bulk. Consider how much you would save by purchasing your meat and veggies in bulk, instead of just buying small portions that you need for one or two meals. You can then prep your meals, and gain all of the other benefits as well. Plus you save money by not making as many different meals, and by avoiding eating out.

❖ It Allows You More Time During The Week

If you're someone who often skips making home cooked meals during the week because you don't have a lot of time due to work and other responsibilities, meal prepping will be perfect for you. Choose an evening or weekend day when you have some extra time, and prepare or cook most of the meals for the week. That way, all that needs to be done is to put your meals together and some minor heating up or cooking the rest of the days of the week.

❖ You Can Eat Healthier

Meal prepping ensures that you will eat healthier meals since every single meal is very carefully planned out. You'll be making multiple healthy meals at one time, often using fresh or frozen produce, lean protein, and other natural ingredients. It also helps you to learn portion control. Use meal prep containers that include compartments that separate different parts of the meals into proper portion sizes.

Preparing your meals ahead of time is not difficult to do. Start by accepting the fact that it will take a bit of time, especially the first time you do it if you've never tried it before.

There may be weeks when you want to include special meals. Maybe you'll want to go through cookbooks and look for recipes online. That's okay. You'll become super organized. You'll have your list of ingredients, so no more realizing as you're cooking that you don't have everything you need.

What Are The Best Ways Of Meal Prepping?
Here are tips for making meal planning (and execution) pain-free.

Don't Go Cold Turkey. If you've been living on takeout and microwaveable meals and your oven haven't been on since the last time you reheated pizza, don't try to tackle it all at once. Start slow, and you won't be as easily overwhelmed and likely to give up.

Make one night your "from scratch" night where you try a new meal that is cooked entirely by you. Make that same meal once a week for a month or two until it becomes second nature. Then start on day two. In between, use items that are semi-prepared to rotate into your repertoire.

Plan for a Month. Don't just plan one week's worth of meals - plan one month. Ok, before you think we've gone completely mad, give us a second. If you make a theme for each day - say Meatless or Mexican Monday, Turkey Tuesday, Wok Wednesday, etc., then all you need to do is find four Mexican recipes for that month, four turkey recipes for that month, etc. and you're all set.

In one planning session, you can plan a month's worth of meals and prep the shopping lists. It takes about 45 minutes if you've never done it before that's not much more time than it takes to plan out a menu for one week if you've never done it before. And having one month's worth of recipes and shopping lists at the ready will keep you on track for much longer.

Sharpen Your Skills. What's the best way to cut your time (literally) in the kitchen? Knife skills. If you know how to properly slice and dice, you'll save yourself a lot of time in the kitchen, so sign up at a local culinary school. Make it date night and your husband will never utter the words.

Plan for the Chaos. We all have crazy weeks, whether you're traveling for work or have two dance recitals and a soccer practice in three days. So look at your calendar for the week and make Sunday your get organized day. You can make some meals ahead of time and freeze them or simply prep the week's meals by cleaning and chopping and store in Ziplocs. What you do today will truly be a lifesaver come midweek.

Buy food in bulk. Save time on grocery shopping by purchasing larger containers/servings of just about everything you buy.

Get larger cooking devices. Sounds silly but it works. Get larger pots, larger baking pans, a larger grill if you have to the more food you can cook at once, the better.

Invest in good Meal Prepping containers. You will need a place to store all the food you're preparing, and nothing is better than Tupperware. Be sure it can go from the fridge to the microwave to the freezer without an issue.

Buy pre-chopped vegetables. If cutting vegetables prevents you from getting these down, buy the pre-chopped variety instead.

Don't overlook frozen vegetables. Or, consider going the frozen vegetable route. You'll never have worries about them staying fresh throughout the week.

Buy convenience for half the process. Okay, so you cannot cook a full-blown meal some days when things are hectic. Why not just modify a meal you buy, so it becomes healthier for you to eat? Try purchasing a frozen dinner for instance and add some of your freshly steamed vegetables to boost the nutritional content. You can make convenience food more healthy much of the time if you make a few small tweaks.

Use your slow cooker. Using a slow cooker is by far the most straightforward and basic way to make healthy eating easy.

Swap cooked food for salads for a few meals during the week. Not only are salads incredibly healthy, but they are also easy to prepare as well. Include them in your eating plan more often.

Snack on fruit. Nothing is easier than smearing a little nut butter on a banana or apple. They are a very healthy and relatively low-calorie fruit to include in your eating plan.

Seek out new recipes. While preparing a fresh new recipe is a bit more work, it's fun, and when it's fun, it won't feel like meal prep.

Keep these ten tips in mind and start applying them to your healthy eating plan. If you do, you can cut the excuse of never having time for meal prep again!

The Common Mistakes Made

❖ **Eating While You Prep**

Tasting here and there is one thing, but mindless snacking just undermines the entire point of meal prep. To ensure you're not overeating during prep time, make sure you've already eaten. Or, work while chewing a stick of gum to be even more cautious.

❖ **Packing The Same Meal Every Day**

While it's easier than dreaming up new meal options for every day, chances are you'll get burnt out on the same grilled chicken on top of a spinach salad for lunch every day.

❖ **Not Cooking At The Right Time**

Like Monday is chest day. Meal prep day is Sunday night or afternoon. Of course, you don't have to follow this rule, but normally this is the best time to do it. It allows you to have an incentive to cook because you want to start next week on the right foot and also most people have Sunday off, and they are relaxed and not under any time pressure to get anything else done. We recommend Sunday but of course, pick any day you wish.

You bought all kinds of food, sealed it up, put it in the closet, and forgot about it. Inevitably, some of the food will become bad, and you will have to throw it out. It's important you store what you eat and eat what you store and rotate your food.

❖ **Not Having Enough Variety In Food Supplies**

Too many new preppers buy nothing but rice, beans, flour, salt, and sugar. If that's all you have to eat, you're going to be miserable. Your body will have trouble adjusting to the new bare-bones diet, and you'll suffer from food fatigue, where your survival food won't be appetizing even when you're very hungry. Make sure you buy the ingredients for a variety of possible meals, so you'll feel satisfied every time you eat.

The Importance Of Balancing The Level Of Proteins, Carbohydrates, And Fats.

Weight loss plans are almost always trying to get you to get rid of some food that you love. However, the three macronutrients (Protein, Carbohydrates, and Fat) as well as the unofficial fourth, water, are all necessary for good health. Never try to eliminate any of these from your diet. If you're trying to lose weight, here is the simple truth about the stuff that makes up food.

Protein Power

Protein is the building block of all life. All life on this planet is made up of amino acids that form chains called proteins. Every function of every cell in your body involves proteins. It should come as no surprise, then, that consuming protein in your diet is essential to your good health.

Protein can come from many sources, not just red meat. All animal parts are protein-rich, from fish to chicken to pork to any animal you'd care to cook up. If you are a vegetarian, you probably already know that many beans and nuts are good sources of protein as well.

The highest concentration of protein is in muscle fibers, in humans and other animals. Therefore, if you want to build up your muscles, you must consume more protein than your minimum daily requirements. And if you consume less than your daily dose, your body may cannibalize your own muscles to get it. This is why an adequate intake of amino acids is essential.

Carbohydrates Cravings

Carbohydrates is a fancy word for something very simple: organic molecules that contain at least two hydrogen atoms for each carbon atom.

All carbohydrates that you can eat are sources of energy. No matter what their composition, your body will break them down into glucose, a simple sugar, which is then used for energy when it is needed. Some carbohydrates are very long chains called "complex carbohydrates," and some are short chains called "simple sugars."

Complex carbs are better for you because they provide more energy, but it takes the body longer to break them apart, which means the energy lasts longer and keeps you feeling full for a longer time. Simple sugars are broken down very quickly, which causes your blood sugar to rise rapidly. If you don't burn it right away, your body will turn it into fat.

Carbohydrates are most abundant in foods that taste sweet. The more delicious the taste, the simpler the carb. So candy of all kinds are made up almost entirely of simple sugars. Carbs are also abundant in fruits and vegetables, as well as grains. Whole grains contain complex carbohydrates, while other grains and plants have shorter chain carbs.

Some modern diets suggest trying to eliminate carbohydrates from your diet because they are a significant source of calories that you're trying to reduce. Reduction of carbs will be necessary for weight loss, but it is of vital importance not to get rid of them altogether.

As mentioned above, carbohydrate-rich foods include fruits and vegetables that contain many vitamins, minerals, antioxidants, and fiber. Losing all those good elements would put your body in a very unhealthy place.

On top of that, your body processes carbs to raise blood-sugar, which is essential to your feeling of satiety or feeling full. If you have no carbs, you may easily be overeating fats (see below). Finally, if your body is not using carbs for energy, it will break apart proteins in your food for energy before it breaks down fats. So, you lose the benefits of amino acids you've eaten, which we discussed above.

A good tactic that many people find easy to identify and follow in their diets is to get rid of "empty carbs," meaning carbohydrates that don't provide anything but energy. White bread, potatoes, refined sugar, and candy are empty carbs that you should avoid.

Fat Is Fine (In Small Doses)

The third macronutrient is fat, which is most easily thought of as concentrated carbs. One gram of fat has nine calories, while carbohydrates and protein contain four calories per gram. So, if you are reducing the calories in your diet, reducing fat is the easiest way to lower the total calorie count.

Not all fats are the same, though. Saturated and trans fats raise LDL cholesterol levels, which increases the risk of heart disease. Unsaturated fats (monounsaturated or polyunsaturated) do not increase these "bad cholesterol" levels and are therefore a better choice.

Fats, unfortunately, taste superb. Fats are the major component in toppings and spreads, such as butter, salad dressing, mayonnaise, and cooking oils. Fats are also the ingredient that makes desserts and snacks so tempting, like cookies, cakes, and chips.

Even though some people try to get rid of all fat, some fat in your diet is necessary. Do not try to eliminate it. Fat aids in the absorption of vitamins A, D, E and K. Essential Fatty Acids, namely omega-3 and omega-6, can only be found in certain fats, and it is important to consume some of these on a regular basis. These nutrients aid in the regulation of blood pressure, blood clotting, and immune response.

To get the good fats without an excess of calories, try eating more fish and seafood instead of other meats. Choose margarine instead of butter. When cooking, choose olive oil to grease your skillet.

And the most effective tip read the labels on the foods you're buying. They should list the fat content, and break it down into Saturated and Unsaturated. If unsaturated is not listed, simply choose the food with the least Saturated fat count.

Four Weeks Plan

Day 1

Breakfast: Make-Ahead Egg & Veggie Muffins

Snack: Mini – Banana Pudding

Lunch: Foil Baked Chicken and Broccoli

Snack: No-Bake Workout Bars

Dinner: Clean Eating Chicken Fried Rice

Day 2

Breakfast: Crustless Quiche Loaf

Snack: Peanut Butter-Yogurt Dip

Lunch: No-Mayo Chicken Salad

Snack: Skinny Bell Pepper Chips

Dinner: Grilled Salmon Kebobs

Day 3

Breakfast: Make-Ahead Egg & Veggie Muffins

Snack: Mini – Banana Pudding

Lunch: Foil Baked Chicken and Broccoli

Snack: No-Bake Workout Bars

Dinner: Clean Eating Chicken Fried Rice

Day 4

Breakfast: Crustless Quiche Loaf

Snack: Peanut Butter-Yogurt Dip

Lunch: No-Mayo Chicken Salad

Snack: Skinny Bell Pepper Chips

Dinner: Grilled Salmon Kebobs

Day 5

Breakfast: Applesauce-Spice Muffins

Snack: Oven Baked Zucchini Chips

Lunch: Six-Ingredient Wild Salmon Fillets

Snack: Green Smoothie

Dinner: Clean Eating Vegetable Fritters

Day 6

Breakfast: Applesauce-Spice Muffins

Snack: Mini Strawberry Cheesecake

Lunch: Kale and Roasted Yam Salad

Snack: Coconut Milk Smoothie

Dinner: Tangerine Grilled Tuna

Day 7

Breakfast: Bacon & Egg Breakfast Muffins

Snack: Oven Baked Zucchini Chips

Lunch: Six-Ingredient Wild Salmon Fillets

Snack: Green Smoothie

Dinner: Clean Eating Vegetable Fritters

Week 2:

Day 1	**Day 2**
Breakfast: 5-Ingredient Baked Egg Mushrooms	**Breakfast:** Avocado Egg Bake Recipe
Snack: Peanut Butter-Yogurt Dip	**Snack:** Mini Apple Cheesecakes
Lunch: Chicken Breasts with Asparagus	**Lunch:** Curried Sweet Potato Soup
Snack: Spinach and Mango Smoothie	**Snack:** Kale & Orange Smoothie
Dinner: Tangerine Grilled Tuna	**Dinner:** Quinoa Stir-Fry
Day 3	**Day 4**
Breakfast: 5-Ingredient Baked Egg Mushrooms	**Breakfast:** Avocado Egg Bake Recipe
Snack: Peanut Butter-Yogurt Dip	**Snack:** Mini Apple Cheesecakes
Lunch: Chicken Breasts with Asparagus	**Lunch:** Curried Sweet Potato Soup
Snack: Spinach and Mango Smoothie	**Snack:** Kale & Orange Smoothie
Dinner: Tangerine Grilled Tuna	**Dinner:** Quinoa Stir-Fry
Day 5	**Day 6**
Breakfast: Banana Walnut Overnight Oatmeal	**Breakfast:** Applesauce-Spice Muffins
Lunch: Kale and Sausage Soup	**Lunch:** No-Mayo Chicken Salad
Snack: Super Green Detox Drink	**Snack:** Pumpkin Spice Smoothie
Dinner: Easy One-Pot Chicken & Rice	**Dinner:** Grilled Salmon Kebobs
Snack: No-Bake Workout Bars	**Snack:** Oven Baked Zucchini Chips

Day 7

Breakfast: Banana Walnut Overnight Oatmeal

Snack: No-Bake Workout Bars

Lunch: Kale and Sausage Soup

Snack: Super Green Detox Drink

Dinner: Easy One-Pot Chicken & Rice

Week 3:

Day 1

Breakfast: Crustless Quiche Loaf

Snack: Oven Baked Zucchini Chips

Lunch: Skillet Chicken and Veggies

Snack: Spinach and Mango Smoothie

Dinner: Clean Eating Chicken Fried Rice

Day 2

Breakfast: Avocado Egg Bake Recipe

Snack: Bell Pepper Nacho Boats

Lunch: Six-Ingredient Wild Salmon Fillets

Snack: Coconut Milk Smoothie

Dinner: Quinoa Stir-Fry

Day 3

Breakfast: Crustless Quiche Loaf

Snack: Oven Baked Zucchini Chips

Lunch: Skillet Chicken and Veggies

Snack: Spinach and Mango Smoothie

Dinner: Clean Eating Chicken Fried Rice

Day 4

Breakfast: Avocado Egg Bake Recipe

Snack: Bell Pepper Nacho Boats

Lunch: Six-Ingredient Wild Salmon Fillets

Snack: Coconut Milk Smoothie

Dinner: Quinoa Stir-Fry

Day 5

Breakfast: Egg & Spinach Bell Pepper Bowls

Snack: Clean-Eating Deviled Eggs

Lunch: Kale and Roasted Yam Salad

Snack: Green Smoothie

Dinner: Indian Chicken and Rice

Day 6

Breakfast: Crustless Quiche Loaf

Snack: Mini – Banana Pudding

Lunch: Skillet Chicken and Veggies

Snack: Kale & Orange Smoothie

Dinner: Herb Crusted Turkey Breast

Day 7

Breakfast: Egg & Spinach Bell Pepper Bowls

Snack: Clean-Eating Deviled Eggs

Lunch: Kale and Roasted Yam Salad

Snack: Green Smoothie

Dinner: Indian Chicken and Rice

Week 4:

Day 1

Breakfast: Egg & Veggie Muffins

Snack: Mini Apple Cheesecakes

Lunch: No-Mayo Chicken Salad

Snack: Pumpkin Spice Smoothie

Dinner: Grilled Salmon Kebobs

Day 2

Breakfast: Banana Walnut Overnight Oatmea

Snack: Coconut Mango Ice Cream

Lunch: Curried Sweet Potato Soup

Snack: Super Green Detox Drink

Dinner: Easy One-Pot Chicken & Rice

Day 3

Breakfast: Egg & Veggie Muffins

Snack: Mini Apple Cheesecakes

Lunch: No-Mayo Chicken Salad

Snack: Pumpkin Spice Smoothie

Dinner: Grilled Salmon Kebobs

Day 4

Breakfast: Banana Walnut Overnight Oatmeal

Snack: Coconut Mango Ice Cream

Lunch: Curried Sweet Potato Soup

Snack: Super Green Detox Drink

Dinner: Easy One-Pot Chicken & Rice

Day 5

Breakfast: Crustless Quiche Loaf

Snack: Strawberry Cheesecake

Lunch: Kale and Roasted Yam Salad

Snack: Coconut Milk Smoothie

Dinner: Quinoa Stir-Fry

Day 6

Breakfast: Egg & Veggie Muffins

Snack: Peanut Butter-Yogurt Dip

Lunch: Skillet Chicken and Veggies

Snack: Kale & Orange Smoothie

Dinner: Potatoes with Crispy Kale and Feta

Day 7

Breakfast: Crustless Quiche Loaf

Snack: Strawberry Cheesecake

Lunch: Kale and Roasted Yam Salad

Snack: Coconut Milk Smoothie

Dinner: Quinoa Stir-Fry

Make-Ahead Egg & Veggie Muffins

Sneak vegetable servings into muffins! My Make-Ahead Egg & Veggie Muffins are light, fluffy, and pack in loads of nutrient-rich veggies. The gluten-free recipe gets the bulk of its texture from eggs and calls for a spectrum of tasty vegetables like juicy bell peppers and zucchini.

Clean ingredients are folded into muffin cups and topped with a sprinkle of cheese, which adds gooey deliciousness to the eggy delights. These highly-portable muffins make a perfect on-the-go breakfast or protein-packed workout snack. Grab and enjoy.

Make muffins ahead of time by freezing in a gallon zip lock bag or freezer safe container. Be sure cupcakes are cooled before freezing. Allow to thaw overnight in the fridge, pop in the 350-degree oven for a few minutes, and enjoy.

Yields: 6 servings, Serving Size: 2 mini muffins or 1 larger muffin per serving, Calories: 118, Total Fat: 8g, Saturated Fat: 3g, Trans Fat: 0g, Cholesterol: 196mg, Sodium: 328mg, Carbohydrates: 2g, Fiber: 1g, Sugar: 1g, Protein: 9g, SmartPoints: 4

Ingredients:

- ❖ 6 large eggs (free-range recommended)
- ❖ 1/2 diced red bell pepper
- ❖ 1 cup diced zucchini
- ❖ 1/4 cup finely diced onion
- ❖ 1/2 teaspoon kosher or sea salt

- ❖ 1/4 teaspoon black pepper
- ❖ 1/2 cup grated cheddar cheese, reduced-fat cheddar cheese

Instructions:

- ❖ Preheat oven to 375 degrees.
- ❖ Lightly oil a 12-cup mini muffin tin or 6-cup tin for regular size muffins.
- ❖ In a mixing bowl, whisk together eggs, bell pepper, zucchini, onion, cheese, and salt and pepper, until light and fluffy.
- ❖ Pour batter into muffin cups, filling each tin about 3/4 full. Sprinkle an even amount of cheese onto each bread. Bake for 15-20 minutes or until eggs is set. Enjoy!

Crustless Quiche Loaf

For an elegant egg-based recipe bursting with flavor, check out this Crustless Quiche Loaf recipe! Traditionally, quiches are baked into a flaky piecrust.

But this buttery base comes at the price of a boatload of calories. The crust is ditched in this recipe, slashing a bunch of excess calories without sacrificing finger-lickin' flavor.

Super simple to make, this quiche calls for a bunch of fresh ingredients like eggs, juicy tomatoes, diced bell pepper, and garden-fresh thyme. This protein-packed meal makes a great brunch dish or a quick dinner on busy weeknights. Once baked, the loaves sport a fluffy texture and offer a colorful presentation that looks beautiful when sliced and served.

Yields: 8 servings, Calories: 97, Total Fat: 5g, Saturated Fat: 2g, Trans Fat: 0g, Cholesterol: 143mg, Sodium: 300mg, Carbohydrates: 3g, Fiber: 1g, Sugar: 2g, Protein: 9g, SmartPoints: 5

Ingredients:

- ❖ 6 egg large egg whites (save yolks if desired)
- ❖ 6 large eggs, whole
- ❖ 1/2 teaspoon baking soda
- ❖ 1/4 cup low-fat milk
- ❖ 2 medium tomatoes, chopped
- ❖ 1 yellow, red, or orange bell pepper, stemmed, seeded, and diced

- ❖ 2 tablespoons fresh thyme leaves
- ❖ 1 cup (part-skim) shredded Mozzarella
- ❖ 1/4 teaspoon kosher or sea salt
- ❖ 1/4 teaspoon black pepper

Instructions:

- ❖ Preheat oven to 350 degrees.
- ❖ Lightly oil a 9 x 5-inch loaf pan. Whisk together 1/2 cup mozzarella and all other ingredients (except tomatoes) until combined. Add tomatoes and gently toss to combine. Pour mixture into prepared loaf pan and sprinkle with remaining mozzarella.
- ❖ Bake for 25 minutes, or until set. A toothpick inserted in the center should come out clean. Cut into slices to serve. Enjoy!

Applesauce-Spice Muffins

I love good baked goods. You know, the tasty treats that would expand your waistline and burden you with frightening amounts of sugar, reinvented in ways that offer nutrients and won't compromise your weight loss goals.

When it comes to nutritious oven-baked treats, these best Applesauce-Spice Muffins top the charts!

Moist and mouthwatering, these muffins make a filling on-the-go breakfast or sweet-tooth satisfier when those sugar cravings are calling.

Yields: 18 servings, Calories: 218, Total Fat: 6g, Saturated Fat: 4g, Trans Fat: 0g, Cholesterol: 22mg, Sodium: 261mg, Carbohydrates: 39g, Fiber: 4g, Sugar: 29g, Protein: 4g, SmartPoints: 11

Ingredients:

- ❖ 2 1/2 cups white whole wheat
- ❖ 1 2/3 cup coconut palm sugar
- ❖ 1 1/2 teaspoons baking soda
- ❖ 1 teaspoon sea salt
- ❖ 1/4 teaspoon baking powder
- ❖ 1 teaspoon cinnamon
- ❖ 1/2 teaspoon cloves
- ❖ 1/2 teaspoon allspice
- ❖ 1 cup diced walnut pieces
- ❖ 1 apple, cored, peeled, and diced into 1/4-inch pieces, (Gala or Golden Delicious, are good choices)
- ❖ 2 eggs, beaten
- ❖ 1/2 cup Greek yogurt
- ❖ 1 1/2 cups applesauce, no sugar added
- ❖ 1 teaspoon pure vanilla
- ❖ 1/3 cup coconut oil

Instructions:

- ❖ Preheat oven to 350 degrees.
- ❖ Place paper or foil muffin cups in muffin tins. In a large mixing bowl, together with all dry ingredients.
- ❖ Add walnuts and toss with dry ingredients.
- ❖ Add remaining ingredients in another medium bowl, whisking until combined. Pour wet ingredients into dry and stir just until combined. Fill 18 muffin cups 2/3 full and bake 20 minutes, or until a toothpick inserted comes out clean.
- ❖ Allow muffins to cool before serving. These muffins are even better the second day.

Bacon & Egg Breakfast Muffins

Baked egg breakfast muffins seem to be all the rage right now. And why wouldn't they be? What a great way cut the carbs by getting rid of toast or English muffins!

These muffins can be made ahead and reheated as a quick breakfast on busy mornings, or taken to a brunch with friends. They're an excellent source of protein and will keep you full and satisfied all morning long.

Yields: 6 servings, Calories: 168, Total Fat: 10g, Saturated Fat: 5g, Trans Fat: 0g, Cholesterol: 214mg, Sodium: 614mg, Carbohydrates: 3g, Fiber: 0g, Sugar: 1g, Protein: 16g, SmartPoints: 5

Ingredients:

- ❖ 4 large eggs
- ❖ 4 slices of diced Canadian bacon (pre-cooked and nitrate-free)
- ❖ 1/2 cup of red bell pepper, diced
- ❖ 1/4 cup of onion, finely diced
- ❖ 1/2 cup of grated low-fat sharp cheddar cheese
- ❖ 1/2 teaspoon of kosher or sea salt
- ❖ 1/4 teaspoon of black pepper
- ❖ 1 tablespoon of vegetable or coconut oil

Instructions:

- ❖ Preheat the oven to 375°F and lightly oil a 6-cup muffin tin with vegetable or coconut oil.
- ❖ In a mixing bowl, whisk together eggs, Canadian bacon, red bell pepper, onion, and sharp cheddar. Season with salt and pepper.
- ❖ Divide the batter among 6 muffin cups and bake for 15-20 minutes, or until eggs are puffy and set.

5-Ingredient Baked Egg Mushrooms

Tired of ordinary egg recipes? Check out this Baked Egg Mushrooms dish, featuring the much-loved portobello mushroom. I adore portobello mushrooms for their meaty texture and their light and healthy nutritional profile. When mushrooms team up with eggs, the two superfoods make a dominant pair in the flavor department.

This oh-so-simple recipe calls for a mere five ingredients, four of which you probably already have in your kitchen. Just crack an egg into each mushroom cap, sprinkle some salt and pepper, and pop in the oven. After about 10 minutes, you have yourself a delicious egg dish. Tender, protein-packed eggs pair beautifully with the juicy texture of the mushrooms.

Yields: 4 servings, Calories: 122, Total Fat: 10g, Saturated Fat: 2g, Trans Fat: 0g, Cholesterol: 186mg, Sodium: 363mg, Carbohydrates: 1g, Fiber: 0g, Sugar: 1g, Protein: 7g, SmartPoints: 4

Ingredients:

- ❖ 4 large portobello mushrooms, cleaned, stems removed and discarded
- ❖ 4 large eggs
- ❖ 1 1/2 tablespoons extra-virgin olive oil
- ❖ 1/2 teaspoon kosher or sea salt, divided
- ❖ 1/2 teaspoon black pepper, divided

Instructions:

- ❖ Preheat oven to 450 degrees.
- ❖ Clean mushrooms with a damp towel paper towel. Rub mushroom caps with olive oil and half the salt and pepper. Place on a baking sheet.
- ❖ Crack an egg carefully into each mushroom cap. Sprinkle each with remaining salt and pepper.
- ❖ Bake for 12-15 minutes until whites of eggs have set and mushrooms have become tender.
- ❖ If desired, sprinkle eggs with green onions and fresh dill. Enjoy.

Egg & Spinach Bell Pepper Bowls

They're easy to prepare and remove lots of empty calories by replacing bread or chips with a hearty veggie. Egg & Spinach Bell Pepper Bowls are no exception. Better yet, they feature deliciously crumbly feta cheese.

These egg bowls are beyond simple to make. You'll come back to them again and again, either for a simple weekday breakfast for part of an elaborate weekend brunch. You can even enjoy them as breakfast for dinner. Dig in and enjoy.

Yields: 2 servings, Calories: 143, Total Fat: 9g, Saturated Fat: 4g, Trans Fat: 0g, Cholesterol: 203mg, Sodium: 493mg, Carbohydrates: 5g, Fiber: 2g, Sugar: 3g, Protein: 10g, SmartPoints: 5

Ingredients:

- ❖ 2 large eggs, (recommend free-range)
- ❖ 4 tablespoons feta cheese crumbles
- ❖ 1/2 teaspoon fresh ground black pepper
- ❖ 1/4 teaspoon Kosher or sea salt
- ❖ 1 cup loosely packed baby spinach, coarsely chopped
- ❖ 1 medium sweet red bell pepper, sliced in half and seeded

Instructions:

- ❖ Preheat oven to 350 degrees F.
- ❖ Break eggs and add to a blender along with salt and pepper. Pulse until combined and fluffy.
- ❖ Add baby spinach, 2 tablespoons feta, and stir to combine. Pour into pepper halves. Sprinkle on remaining cheese and a little more black pepper.
- ❖ Place filled peppers next to each other, in a small casserole dish, so they are snug and won't spill. Bake until eggs puff and are set, 15-20 minutes
- ❖ Enjoy.

Egg and Toast Breakfast Cups Recipes

These delicious egg and toast cups shake up breakfast! This recipe puts a brilliant twist on two breakfast staples. All you have to do is shape bread slices into muffin cups and crack an egg in each round. Once baked to perfection, you'll have warm, crunchy toast cradling a fluffy egg.

This dish is an excellent source of protein for any diet. Add a layer of cheddar cheese for a gooey, mouthwatering touch, or a slice of lean turkey if you have morning meat cravings. Vegetarians still get plenty of nutrients from the eggs without sacrificing any flavor. Even your breakfast-skipping friends will savor these light and fluffy Egg and Toast Breakfast Cups.

Yields: 6 servings, Serving Size: 1 cup, Calories: 278, Total Fat: 16g, Saturated Fat: 5g, Trans Fat: 0g, Cholesterol: 224mg, Sodium: 401mg, Carbohydrates: 13g, Fiber: 2g, Sugar: 1g, Protein: 21g, SmartPoints: 8

Ingredients:

- ❖ 6 slices whole wheat bread, crusts removed
- ❖ 3 slices nitrate-free deli turkey or vegan turkey substitute, sliced in half, (optional)
- ❖ 1/2 cup grated reduced fat cheddar cheese, (optional)
- ❖ 6 large eggs
- ❖ 2 tablespoons olive oil
- ❖ 1/4 teaspoon kosher or sea salt
- ❖ 1/4 teaspoon black pepper
- ❖

Instructions:

- ❖ Note that turkey and cheese are both optional ingredients. This recipe can be made with just eggs and toast if desired.
- ❖ Preheat oven to 375 degrees. Spray 6 cups in a muffin tin with cooking spray or lightly grease with olive oil. Gently press each slice of bread into a round. Fold over and press edges of dough to fit in the muffin cup, if necessary.
- ❖ Brush each slice of bread with olive oil. The back of a spoon can be used if you do not have a pastry or basting brush. Sprinkle the bottom of each cup with cheddar cheese, if using. Add a layer of turkey, folded over to fit if using.
- ❖ Crack an egg into each bread round. Sprinkle with salt and pepper. Bake for about 20 minutes, until the whites of the eggs are set. Serve and enjoy.

Avocado Egg Bake Recipe

Though many people believe that high-fat foods make you gain weight, foods that contain essential fatty acids have been linked to weight loss and good heart health. Your diet should include foods with omega-3 and omega-6 to maintain a healthy lifestyle.

For a low-carb breakfast full of healthy fats, try this Avocado Egg Bake! Avocados are one of the world's healthiest foods. They provide fiber, omega-3s, and a variety of minerals. Eggs contain a right balance of fats and protein. The combination of avocado and eggs is not only delicious but incredibly healthy as well.

Yields: 2 servings, Serving Size: 1/2 avocado, Calories: 233, Total Fat: 20g, Saturated Fat: 4g, Trans Fat: 0g, Cholesterol: 186mg, Sodium: 369mg, Carbohydrates: 9g, Fiber: 7g, Sugar: 1g, Protein: 8g, SmartPoints: 8

Ingredients:

- ❖ 1 ripe avocado
- ❖ 2 eggs, organic free-range
- ❖ 2 pinches freshly ground black pepper
- ❖ 2 pinches kosher or sea salt
- ❖ 2 pinches paprika
- ❖ 4 fresh rosemary leaves, cut into small pieces

Instructions:

- ❖ Preheat oven to 400 degrees.
- ❖ Cut the avocado in half, remove the pit, and scoop out (and discard) about two teaspoons from each half to make room for the eggs. Crack open one egg at a time and drop into each avocado half, making sure the yolk is in the center of each half.
- ❖ Season each egg with black pepper, salt, paprika, and sliced rosemary leaves.Carefully transfer each avocado half to a parchment lined baking pan. Place in the oven. Allow to bake for 10 minutes or until the whites have set. Remove from the oven and enjoy.

Eggs With Mushrooms &Brussels Sprouts

It's Sunday morning, and everyone's clamoring for food. They want something that hasn't been done a million times before; a fried egg dish with some pizzazz. Fear not! Instead of boring old eggs and toast, whip out your trusty Fried Eggs with Mushrooms & Brussels Sprouts recipe and your Sunday morning brunch will never be boring again.

This fried egg dish boasts four full cups of halved Brussels sprouts. The party only gets more scrumptious with an entire pint of baby Bella mushrooms. Garlic, onion and toasted walnuts combine forces to create an unbeatable flavor sensation. So next time Sunday brunch rolls around and you're in charge of the fried egg dish, relax. You've got it covered.

Yields: 4 servings, Calories: 189, Total Fat: 13 g, Saturated Fat: 3 g, Trans Fat: 0 g, Sodium: 241 mg, Cholesterol: 186 mg, Carbohydrates: 10 g, Fiber: 4 g, Sugars: 3 g, Protein: 10 g, SmartPoints: 6

Ingredients:

- ❖ 4 large eggs
- ❖ 4 cups brussels sprouts, halved
- ❖ 2 tablespoons olive oil
- ❖ 1-pint baby Bella mushrooms, smaller ones halved and larger ones quartered
- ❖ 1/2 cup chopped onions
- ❖ 1 clove garlic, minced
- ❖ 3 tablespoons vegetable stock or water
- ❖ 1/4 teaspoon kosher or sea salt
- ❖ 1/4 teaspoon black pepper
- ❖ 1/4 cup walnuts, toasted and coarsely chopped
- ❖ 1 sprig of thyme for garnish (optional)
- ❖ 1/4 cup grated parmesan cheese

Instructions:

In a sauté pan over medium heat, add olive oil, onions, and brussels sprouts and cook for 5 minutes. Add mushrooms, salt, and pepper. Cook for 12 more minutes, stirring frequently. Insert the minced garlic, cook for 30 seconds longer. Add the stock. Cook for 3 minutes or until the stock has evaporated. Form 4 spaces between the vegetables. Add eggs to each space. Reduce heat to low and cook for 5 to 8 minutes or until the eggs are cooked through.

Meanwhile, toast the walnuts in a dry skillet over medium heat on another burner for 3 to 5 minutes. Stir frequently, until golden and fragrant. Remove from pan and allow to cool. Once cool enough to handle then coarsely chop. Remove from heat. Sprinkle with walnuts and parmesan. Garnish with thyme, if desired. Enjoy!

Eggs With Spinach And Creamed Feta

Yields: 4 servings, Calories: 134, Total Fat: 8g, Saturated Fat: 3g, Trans Fat: 0g, Carbohydrates: 5g, Fiber: 2g, Sugar: 2g, Sodium: 397mg, Cholesterol: 197 mg, Protein: 11g, SmartPoints: 4

Ingredients:

Eggs And Spinach

- ❖ 4 eggs
- ❖ 1 tablespoon olive oil
- ❖ 1 bunch spinach, cleaned and rough ends of stems removed
- ❖ 2 garlic cloves, thinly sliced
- ❖ 1/4 teaspoon salt, divided
- ❖ 1/4 teaspoon pepper, divided

Creamed Feta Sauce

- ❖ 1/4 cup crumbled feta
- ❖ 1/4 cup low-fat plain Greek yogurt

Instructions:

Add olive oil to a sauté pan or skillet over medium heat. Add the spinach, garlic, and half the salt and pepper. Sauté spinach for two minutes, until thoroughly wilted, and make four egg-sized spaces in the spinach to crack eggs into. Add the eggs to each space and sprinkle them with the remaining salt and pepper.

Cook for two to three minutes until the egg whites are solid, but the yolks are still soft and gooey.Meanwhile, blend the feta and yogurt in the blender. Serve eggs and spinach with the creamed feta sauce.

Strawberry, Almond Butter, And Oatmeal Breakfast Parfait

This combination of fresh fruit blended into a creamy smoothie and tasty oatmeal is an almost dessert-style concoction that is good for you. Frozen bananas and sliced strawberries are blended into an ice cream-like smoothie and then layered with hot oats flavored with almond butter for an out of this world treat that is both decadent and delicious.
Make sure your oats are warm, but not piping hot when you put this together; otherwise, they will melt the banana and strawberry mixture.

Yields: 2 servings, Serving Size: 1 cup, Calories: 332, Total Fat: 13 g, Saturated Fat: 7 g, Trans Fat: 0 g, Cholesterol: 10 mg, Sodium: 11 mg, Carbohydrates: 49 g, Dietary Fiber: 12 g, Sugars: 19 g, Protein: 7 g, SmartPoints: 14

Ingredients:

- ❖ 1/2 cup rolled oats
- ❖ 1 cup water
- ❖ 1/4 cup almond milk
- ❖ 1 teaspoon vanilla
- ❖ 1 tablespoon almond butter
- ❖ 2 frozen bananas
- ❖ 1 cup sliced strawberries
- ❖ Sliced almonds and strawberries, for garnish

Instructions:

Combine the oats and water in a saucepan and cook over low heat for 5-6 minutes. Stir in the almond milk, vanilla, and almond butter. Stir until almond butter is melted. Turn off heat and allow to cool slightly.

When the oats are slightly warm, but not hot, put the bananas and strawberries in a blender. Blend, pushing ingredients down with a tamper if necessary. Add a tablespoon or two of almond milk to help blend if needed, being careful not to add too much (it should be very thick, almost like ice cream.)

To serve, layer the warm oats with the frozen strawberry mixture in a jar or parfait glass. Top with sliced almonds and strawberries and eat with a spoon.

Banana Walnut Overnight Oatmeal

Overnight oats are trending these days and for a good reason. Instead of lingering by the stove waiting for oats to simmer and thicken, prepare this overnight oatmeal by throwing ingredients into a jar and popping it in the refrigerator.

Oats absorb milk and flavor from added spices overnight, forming a deliciously creamy grab-and-go breakfast.

This recipe packs the mouthwatering goodness of a banana walnut muffin into an uber-nutritious oatmeal. Raw honey and a dash of cinnamon add pleasant sweetness, while chia seeds bump up the fiber content. Fast and a cinch to prepare, this no-cook, no-bake morning meal will get you up and keep you going all day long!

Yields: 2 servings, Calories: 213, Total Fat: 5g, Saturated Fat: 1g, Trans Fat: 0g, Cholesterol: 6mg, Sodium: 117mg, Carbohydrates: 38g, Fiber: 3g, Sugar: 28g, Protein: 7g, SmartPoints: 9

Ingredients:

Oats

- ❖ 1/3 cup rolled oats
- ❖ 1/2 cup low-fat milk
- ❖ 1/3 cup plain low-fat yogurt
- ❖ 1 tablespoon honey
- ❖ 1/4 teaspoon ground cinnamon
- ❖ 1/4 teaspoon vanilla extract
- ❖ Pinch sea salt

For serving

- ❖ 1/4 cup chopped walnuts
- ❖ 1 banana, peeled and sliced

Instructions:

Add all of the ingredients to two bowls or jars, cover, and stir to combine. Refrigerate for 6-8 hours.

When ready to serve, heat the oats in the microwave or enjoy chilled. Top with the walnuts and banana slices just before serving.

LUNCH RECIPES

No-Mayo Chicken The Salad

This dish is a summertime favorite because chicken salad never fails to impress. However, mayonnaise plays a significant role in standard recipes, contributing to the dish's high-calorie profile. Just one tablespoon of mayo clocks in at a frightening 100 calories and most recipes call for a lot more than a single tablespoon.

People fear ditching the caloric condiment, assuming its absence would compromise the creamy, indulgent flavor of their favorite dishes.

Luckily, my No-Mayo Chicken Salad lets you enjoy the scrumptious meal without worrying about your waistline! Olive oil combines with a splash of lemon juice, to add texture and a bunch of incredible nutrients.

Chopped celery and lettuce add a delicate crunch, while cherry tomatoes offer some juicy goodness your taste buds will love. This healthy dish is a snap to make and guaranteed to satisfy.

Yields: 6 servings, Calories: 217, Total Fat: 16g, Saturated Fat: 3g, Trans Fat: 0g, Cholesterol: 48mg, Sodium: 442mg, Carbohydrates: 2g, Fiber: 0g, Sugar: 1g, Protein: 16g, SmartPoints: 6

Ingredients:

- ❖ 1 pound chicken breast, cut into bite-size pieces
- ❖ 1/4 cup extra-virgin olive oil
- ❖ 3 tablespoons lemon juice
- ❖ 1/4 teaspoon kosher or sea salt, more to taste
- ❖ 1/4 teaspoon black pepper
- ❖ 1 cup cherry tomatoes, halved or quartered
- ❖ 1/2 cup diced celery
- ❖ 1 tablespoon freshly chopped dill or 1 teaspoon dried
- ❖ 1/4 cup freshly chopped parsley
- ❖ 6 large savory (curly) cabbage leaves for serving, optional iceberg lettuce

Instructions:

- ❖ In a large skillet over medium heat, add 1 tablespoon olive oil, sauté chicken until golden brown.
- ❖ While cooking the chicken, in a small bowl, mix remaining 3 tablespoon olive oil, lemon juice, salt, and pepper. After chicken turns golden, transfer to a serving bowl and toss with tomatoes, celery, dill, and parsley. Drizzle with dressing and combine, or serve on the side. Enjoy it!

Foil Baked Chicken And Broccoli

What's the best thing about this Foil Baked Chicken and Broccoli? There's a three-way tie between how delicious it is, how healthy it is, and how easy it is to clean up. You don't need the stovetop for this filling, nutrient-packed dinner. Plus, the only dish you will need to use is a baking sheet to put the foil packets on.

Unlike other chicken and broccoli recipes, my requires no oil, butter or any other ingredients that typically increase the fat or calorie count. Instead, a simple mix of spices creates tons of flavor, and you get your veggies and meat in one easy packet. What could be better?

Yields: 2 servings, Calories: 292, Total Fat: 14g, Saturated Fat: 4g, Trans Fat: 0g, Cholesterol: 64mg, Sodium: 181mg, Carbohydrates: 22g, Fiber: 8g, Sugar: 5g, Protein: 25g, SmartPoints:8

Ingredients:

- ❖ 1 head broccoli, top cut into medium florets
- ❖ 4 tablespoons water
- ❖ 2 boneless and skinless free-range chicken breast
- ❖ 1 clove garlic, smashed and minced
- ❖ 1/2 teaspoon dry thyme
- ❖ 1/4 teaspoon ground rosemary
- ❖ 1/2 teaspoon ground sage
- ❖ Kosher salt
- ❖ Ground black pepper

Instructions:

- ❖ Preheat oven to 375 degrees F.
- ❖ Lightly spray two large pieces of foil with nonstick spray. Leaving space around the edges to roll later, place half the broccoli on each piece. Drizzle two tablespoons of water on each pile of broccoli.
- ❖ On top of the broccoli, place chicken breast. Sprinkle remaining ingredients on top of chicken.
- ❖ Carefully fold in sides of foil sheet to cover chicken and place on cookie sheet. Bake 15 to 20 minutes until chicken reaches an internal temperature of 165 degrees F and no pink remains.
- ❖ Before unfolding foil, carefully cut slits into the pack to release steam. Once the steam has been released, reveal and enjoy.

Skillet Chicken And Veggies

The savory aroma of this Skillet Chicken and Veggies sizzling in your pan will pervade your kitchen and make dinner guests go wild. Packed with clean, wholesome ingredients, this pure, protein-rich dish is the perfect staple to add to your cookbook.

These nutritional properties make quite a treasure chest of health benefits. Tender, crispy chicken meets juicy carrots and deliciously smooth potatoes in this skillet dish. The meat packs a protein punch while the veggies offer incredible nutrients like Vitamin B6, potassium, copper, and Vitamin C.

You only need one skillet to whip up this easy dish. It allows for no-stress prep and minimum clean up while yielding a wholesome meal with maximum flavor.

Yields: 4 servings, Calories: 240, Total Fat: 7g, Saturated Fat: 2g, Trans Fat: 0g, Cholesterol: 45mg, Sodium: 374mg, Carbohydrates: 27g, Fiber: 3g, Sugar: 5g, Protein: 18g, SmartPoints: 7

Ingredients:

- ❖ 2 chicken breast fillets, cut into bite-size pieces
- ❖ 2 tablespoons extra-virgin olive oil
- ❖ 1 onion, coarsely chopped
- ❖ 1 medium red potato, peeled and diced
- ❖ 1 large carrot, peeled and thinly sliced
- ❖ 1 garlic, minced
- ❖ 1 tablespoon balsamic vinegar
- ❖ 1/4 cup freshly chopped basil
- ❖ 1 tablespoon fresh thyme leaves
- ❖ 1/2 teaspoon kosher or sea salt
- ❖ 1/4 teaspoon black pepper
- ❖ 2 tablespoons chopped Italian parsley, for garnish

Instructions:

- ❖ In a large saucepan add olive oil, over medium heat sauté chicken pieces until lightly golden. Add onion, potatoes and, carrots and continue cooking until tender and chicken are cooked through.
- ❖ Add garlic, vinegar, herbs, salt, and pepper, and sauté for 1 additional minutes.
- ❖ Sprinkle with parsley before serving. Enjoy.

Four-Ingredient Roasted Cauliflower

When it comes to whipping up something delicious, you can't go wrong with roasting. One of my all-time favorite cooking methods, roasting cranks up the flavor of a variety of foods. This scrumptious roasted cauliflower recipe takes the flavor of a basic cruciferous vegetable to a whole new level.

Eating vegetables have never tasted so good! Once you've bitten into these irresistibly crispy cauliflower florets, you'll never go back to boiling. This rocking recipe calls for just four ingredients, slashing a ton of meal prep time and allowing you to dish up something nutritious without stress. Simply toss florets with olive oil, sprinkle some salt and pepper, and pop in the oven. These roasted florets make a scrumptious side dish and a clever way to sneak more veggies into your diet.

Yields: 6 servings, Calories: 41, Total Fat: 4g, Saturated Fat: 1g, Trans Fat: 0g, Cholesterol: 0mg, Sodium: 207mg, Carbohydrates: 2g, Fiber: 1g, Sugar: 1g, Protein: 1g, SmartPoints: 2

Ingredients:

- ❖ 1 head cauliflower, cut into florets
- ❖ 3 tablespoons extra-virgin olive oil
- ❖ 1/2 teaspoon kosher or sea salt
- ❖ 1/2 teaspoon black pepper

Instructions:

- ❖ Preheat oven to 425 degrees.
- ❖ Toss cauliflower with olive oil, salt, and pepper to coat. Spread in an even layer on a baking sheet. Bake for 20 to 25 minutes on middle oven rack, stirring halfway through, until golden and crispy.

Six-Ingredient Wild Salmon Fillets

Whipping up a fish dinner makes you feel like you're swimming against the current. Seafood meals are easier than you think, especially with this tasty Wild Salmon Fillets recipe! With just six simple ingredients and 15-minute prep time, this recipe makes cooking salmon at home a snap.

Rich in omega-3s and heart-healthy vitamins, salmon, adds an incredible dose of nutrients to any meal. The fabulous fish also boosts your mood, improves your skin, and contributes to healthy nervous system functioning.

After baking, this salmon offers a soft, buttery texture that simply melts in your mouth. These fillets serve as a blank canvas for a host of seasonings and sauces. Drizzled with olive oil and baked with juicy cherry tomatoes, this mouthwatering fish recipe will satisfy your taste buds and become a regular in your house.

Yields: 4 servings, Calories: 367, Total Fat: 22g, Saturated Fat: 5g, Trans Fat: 0g, Cholesterol: 70mg, Sodium: 368mg, Carbohydrates: 15g, Fiber: 1g, Sugar: 12g, Protein: 27g, SmartPoints: 11

Ingredients:

- ❖ 4 (4-5 ounce) wild salmon fillets with skin on
- ❖ 1 1/2 tablespoons extra-virgin olive oil
- ❖ 2 cups grape or cherry tomatoes
- ❖ 1 lemon, rinsed and sliced
- ❖ 1/2 teaspoon kosher or sea salt
- ❖ 1/2 teaspoon black pepper

Instructions:

- ❖ Preheat oven to 450 degrees.
- ❖ Add salmon fillets to a baking dish, skin-side down. Rub top and sides of salmon with olive oil and sprinkle with salt and pepper. Top with lemon slices.
- ❖ Add tomatoes around fish. Bake for 8 to 10 minutes, just until fish is firm and flakes easily with a fork. Enjoy!

Lemon Chicken Breasts With Asparagus & Salad

My Lemon Chicken Breasts with Salad & Asparagus recipe delivers fresh, summery flavors in every bite. It's the perfect family meal in any season! The meal features three main components: chicken, asparagus, and salad. Chopped rosemary sprigs and thyme give the chicken a garden-fresh kick.

The savory herbs pair well with my tangy olive oil and lemon juice mixture. Luscious asparagus spears roast to tender-brown perfection and gorgeously complement the juicy chicken. Finish by tossing a side salad made of greens and tomatoes with a drizzle of bold vinaigrette.

These ultra-nutritious meal pairs lean protein with delicious greens. It's a dish your body and taste buds will adore. Dish up and enjoy.

Yields: 4 servings, Calories: 374, Total Fat: 24g, Saturated Fat: 4g, Trans Fat: 0g, Cholesterol: 83mg, Sodium: 214mg, Carbohydrates: 10g, Fiber: 4g, Sugar: 4g, Protein: 25g, SmartPoints: 11g

Ingredients:

Chicken

- ❖ 1 pound boneless, skinless chicken breasts
- ❖ 3 tablespoons fresh squeezed lemon juice
- ❖ 3 tablespoons olive oil plus 2 teaspoons, divided
- ❖ 4 tablespoons chopped rosemary sprigs
- ❖ 4 tablespoons chopped thyme
- ❖ 2 garlic cloves, minced
- ❖ 1/2 teaspoon crushed red pepper flakes
- ❖ 1/2 teaspoon kosher or sea salt

Asparagus

- ❖ 1 pound asparagus, cleaned and woody bottoms removed (about 1-inch from bottom)
- ❖ 1 tablespoon extra-virgin olive oil
- ❖ 1/4 teaspoon kosher or sea salt
- ❖ 1/4 teaspoon pepper

Salad

- ❖ 4 cups mixed greens
- ❖ 1 cup halved tomatoes
- ❖ 3 tablespoons clean eating vinaigrette of choice, homemade or store bought

Instructions:

For Chicken:

- ❖ Using a meat tenderizer, pound chicken breasts to an even thickness.

- ❖ Whisk together lemon juice, garlic, herbs, salt, pepper, and 3 tablespoons of the olive oil. Marinate chicken and mixture in an airtight container or resealable bag for at least 30 minutes and up to 2 hours.
- ❖ Place 2 teaspoons olive oil in a skillet over medium-high heat. Spread oil and coat the pan. Add chicken. Cook for 1 minute on each side. Flip breasts again and reduce heat to low.
- ❖ Cover pan with a tight-fitting lid. Cook for 10 minutes (check time). Do not remove lid while cooking. After 10 minutes, remove the pan from heat, still covered, and allow to sit for 10 additional minutes.
- ❖ Make sure there is no pink in the middle of the breasts or that a meat thermometer reads 165 F when inserted in the center.
- ❖ Meanwhile, for asparagus: Preheat oven to 400 degrees F.
- ❖ Toss asparagus with olive oil, salt, and pepper. Spread on a sheet tray. Roast for 18-20 minutes, flipping asparagus halfway through until slightly browned and tender.
- ❖ For the salad: Toss greens and tomatoes together. Toss with a vinaigrette of choice or serve to dress on the side. Enjoy.

Mediterranean Grilled Shrimp Entrée Salad

Do you remember your last great beach vacation? Maybe you had the opportunity to visit Italy's shores, and dined al fresco, enjoying fresh vegetable salads topped with luscious shrimp right from the ocean.

Or maybe you toured Northern California or the coast of Florida, and enjoyed crisp, green salads, with in season veggies and that same scrumptious shrimp.

This recipe for Mediterranean Grilled Shrimp Entree Salad, and is reminiscent of the type of coastal Italian fare served up in Italy, or in warm, beachy locales across North America. Now you can delight friends and family with this salad in your kitchen or backyard.

The base of this salad is comprised of ripe, cherry tomatoes, delicious and juicy, combined with tangy sun-dried tomatoes and peppery arugula. But fennel adds its unique flavor, truly Mediterranean, and totally gourmet. Fennel tastes of anise, or licorice, and lends a sweet, surprising twist to any dish. Using both the bulbs and seeds of the fennel plant will enhance this salad, giving it a well-rounded flavor profile.

Yields: 6 servings, Serving Size: 4 jumbo shrimp and 2 cups salad, Calories: 390, Total Fat: 17 g, Saturated Fat: 1 g, Trans Fat: 0 g, Cholesterol: 48 mg, Sodium: 175 mg, Carbohydrates: 52 g, Dietary Fiber: 34 g, Sugars: 7 g, Protein: 20 g, SmartPoints: 11

Ingredients:

- ❖ 24 jumbo shrimp (about 1-1/2 pounds), shelled & deveined
- ❖ 1/2 teaspoon salt + more for sprinkling on the griddle
- ❖ 8 cups arugula
- ❖ 24 sun-dried tomatoes (from a jar, preserved in oil)
- ❖ 2 fennel bulbs, shaved with the use of a mandoline or sliced as thinly as possible with a sharp knife
- ❖ 24 fresh cherry tomatoes, halved
- ❖ 2 lemons, zest only
- ❖ 1/4 teaspoon pepper
- ❖ 2 teaspoons fennel seeds (optional)
- ❖ 2 tablespoons extra virgin olive oil
- ❖ 2 tablespoons balsamic vinegar

Instructions:

- ❖ Over medium - high heat, place an oven-top griddle or a heavy bottomed saucepan with then sprinkle it with salt. Grill the shrimp and brown both sides. Set them aside.
- ❖ Distribute the arugula on the plate then add the fennel, sun-dried tomatoes and fresh tomatoes.
- ❖ Place the grilled shrimp on top then sprinkle with the lemon zest, fennel seeds, salt, and pepper.
- ❖ Dress with the extra virgin olive oil and balsamic vinegar.

Grilled Chicken And Avocado Salad

This salad's complimentary flavors create a delicious, subtle dish with nutrients in every bite. The white meat, which is much healthier than its red counterpart, is grilled simply, rubbed with only extra virgin olive oil and balsamic vinegar. Together, they create an Italian flair. As you throw  together the rest of the ingredients in the bowl, you will inhale the aromatic smell of freshly grilled skinny chicken with balsamic vinegar and avocado.

Yields: 6 servings, Serving Size: 4, Calories: 312, Total Fat: 23 g, Saturated Fat: 3 g, Trans Fat: 0 g, Cholesterol: 48 mg, Sodium: 250 mg, Carbohydrates: 9 g, Dietary Fiber: 5 g, Sugars: 2 g, Protein: 18 g, SmartPoints 9

Ingredients:

- ❖ 1 pound skinless, boneless chicken breast fillet
- ❖ 1 teaspoon salt
- ❖ 1/4 teaspoon ground pepper
- ❖ 1/4 cup extra virgin olive oil
- ❖ 4 tablespoons balsamic vinegar
- ❖ 2 avocados, peeled and sliced
- ❖ 6 cups lettuce or any salad greens

Instructions:

- ❖ Rub the chicken with half of the extra virgin olive oil, half of the salt and all the pepper.
- ❖ Over medium - high heat, on a boiling griddle, grill both sides of the chicken. While cooking, brush each side with half of the balsamic vinegar.
- ❖ When the chicken is cooked, chop them into smaller pieces.
- ❖ In a big salad bowl, mix the salad, avocados, chicken, the remaining extra virgin olive oil, salt and balsamic vinegar.

Kale And Roasted Yam Salad

This Kale and Roasted Yam Salad is far from ordinary. The brightly colored veggie dish calls for unconventional salad foods like sweet potatoes to amp up the flavor. It also uses a bunch of ultra-nutritious superfoods like sesame seeds, pumpkin seeds, and avocado. The yams deliver a hint of sweetness and a buttery

texture that complements the crunchy kale perfectly. The tangy blend of lemon juice and olive oil form a lovely dressing that will excite your taste buds. This vegetarian-friendly, spruced-up kale salad will be a guaranteed favorite among family and friends!

Yields: 4 servings, Serving Size: 2 cups, Calories: 200, Total Fat: 13g, Saturated Fat: 2g, Trans Fat: 0g, Cholesterol: 0mg, Sodium: 52mg, Carbohydrates: 21g, Fiber: 8g, Sugars: 5g, Protein: 6g, SmartPoints: 7

Ingredients:

- ❖ 1 bunch lacinato (also called Tuscan or dinosaur) kale, cleaned, ribs and stems removed and chopped OR 1 10-ounce package baby kale
- ❖ 1 sweet potato, peeled and chopped into 1-inch cubes
- ❖ 1 tablespoon extra virgin olive oil
- ❖ 1 ripe avocado, peeled, pitted and cut into slices
- ❖ 2 teaspoons freshly squeezed lemon or lime juice (about half lemon or lime)
- ❖ 1 tablespoon sesame seeds
- ❖ 1/3 cup pumpkin or shelled sunflower seeds

- ❖ 1 cup (half a pint) cherry or grape tomatoes, halved
- ❖ 1/2 teaspoon kosher or sea salt, divided
- ❖ 1/4 teaspoon black pepper, divided

Instructions:

- ❖ Preheat oven to 375 degrees. Toss sweet potatoes with olive oil, 1/4 teaspoon of the salt, and 1/8 teaspoon pepper. Spread on a parchment-lined or nonstick baking sheet.
- ❖ Roast for 25 minutes, flipping the pieces halfway through, or until fork tender and browned a bit. Add kale, tomatoes, sweet potatoes, remaining 1/4 teaspoon salt, and 1/8 teaspoon black pepper to a salad bowl and toss. Sweet potato pieces may be added warm or cold. Sprinkle the salad with sesame seeds and pumpkin seeds or sunflower seeds.
- ❖ Gently toss avocado slices in lemon/lime juice, and add on top of the salad. Enjoy with your favorite dressing or a simple vinaigrette.

Slow Cooker Italian Chicken And Sweet Potatoes

Most days, you don't want to dirty a bunch of pots and pans just to make a meal. Luckily, my Slow Cooker Italian Chicken and Sweet Potatoes recipe are a one-pot meal for such days. The whole meal is prepared in the slow cooker and allowed to simmer for those amazing flavors to soak in. Olive oil, lemon juice, herbs, and spices give it a

great Italian flavor, and the mushrooms and sweet potatoes make it a hearty meal. Serve the chicken breasts with a spoonful of the mushrooms and sweet potatoes.

Yields: 4 servings, Serving Size: 1 1/2 cups, Calories: 364, Total Fat: 16g, Saturated Fat: 2g, Trans Fat: 0g, Cholesterol: 62mg, Sodium: 700mg, Carbohydrates: 33g, Fiber: 5g, Sugar: 8g, Protein: 24g, SmartPoints: 10

Ingredients:

- ❖ 4 boneless skinless chicken breasts, (optional, 2 pounds of dark meat or a combination)
- ❖ 8 ounces cremini mushrooms, halved
- ❖ 2 cups diced sweet potatoes
- ❖ 1/4 cup fresh lemon juice
- ❖ 1/2 cup chicken broth
- ❖ 1/4 cup olive oil
- ❖ 1 teaspoon dried oregano
- ❖ 1 teaspoon dried parsley
- ❖ 1 teaspoon dried basil
- ❖ 1 teaspoon kosher or sea salt
- ❖ 1/2 teaspoon black pepper
- ❖ 1/2 teaspoon onion powder
- ❖ 2 garlic cloves, minced

Instructions:

- ❖ Place the chicken in the middle of the slow cooker, then put the sweet potatoes on one side and the mushrooms on the other. In another bowl, whisk the remaining ingredients together, then pour over the ingredients in the slow cooker. Cover and cook for 4 to 6 hours on low or 3 to 4 hours on high.

Curried Sweet Potato Soup Recipe

There's nothing quite as comforting as a hot bowl of soup on a chilly night. This curried sweet potato soup recipe blends sweet and spicy for a tantalizing medley of flavors. Made with delicious spices, creamy coconut milk, and a hint of lime juice, it's exotic and comforting all at once.

Preparing your recipe is a breeze. All you have to do is add the ingredients one by one, cook to perfection, top with cilantro and coconut, and serve! The dish makes a perfect complementary side or hearty solo meal. The nutrient-packed, vegetarian ingredient list means the whole family can savor the heavenly flavor.

Yields: 4 servings, Serving Size: 1 cup, Calories: 246, Total Fat: 18 g, Saturated Fat: 9 g, Trans Fat: 0 g, Cholesterol: 0 mg, Sodium: 54 mg, Carbohydrates: 19 g, Dietary Fiber: 5 g, Sugars: 6 g, Protein: 2 g, SmartPoints: 11

Ingredients:

- ❖ 2 tablespoons coconut oil
- ❖ 1 onion, diced
- ❖ 2 cloves garlic
- ❖ 1 large sweet potato, peeled and diced
- ❖ 2 tablespoons curry powder
- ❖ 1/2 teaspoon cumin
- ❖ 1/4 teaspoon cayenne pepper
- ❖ 1/2 teaspoon sea salt
- ❖ 1 15-ounce can light coconut milk

- ❖ Juice of 1 lime
- ❖ 1/4 cup chopped cilantro
- ❖ 1/4 cup shredded coconut

Instructions:

- ❖ Heat coconut oil in a large saucepan or Dutch oven over medium heat.
- ❖ Add onions and cook until soft.
- ❖ Add garlic and cook for about a minute.
- ❖ Add sweet potatoes, stir, and cook for 5 minutes.
- ❖ Stir in spices and cook for about a minute.
- ❖ Add coconut milk.
- ❖ Bring to a simmer over low heat for 20-25 minutes, until sweet potatoes are tender.
- ❖ Using either an immersion blender or regular blender, puree soup until smooth.
- ❖ Transfer back to the pot and add lime juice.
- ❖ Top with chopped cilantro and coconut.

Slow Cooker Kale And Sausage Soup

When the temperature drops, there's nothing better than a bowl of delicious soup to warm you up. But this soup is a standout, with kale and potatoes as the main ingredients. Choose a sausage that delivers lean protein, such as turkey. This healthy and straightforward rustic soup has a slightly creamy consistency, which comes from blitzing half of the soup in the blender. Even when you're watching your calories, you can still enjoy bold flavors in your bowl.

Yields: 4 servings, Serving Size: 1/4 of recipe/ about 2 cups, Calories: 375, Total Fat: 14 g, Saturated Fat: 3 g, Trans Fat: 0 g, Cholesterol: 29 mg, Sodium: 339 mg, Carbohydrates: 48 g, Dietary Fiber: 6 g, Sugars: 5 g, Protein: 16 g, SmartPoints: 11

Instructions:

- ❖ 3 turkey sausages, sliced (nitrate-free)
- ❖ 3 cups chopped kale
- ❖ 2 medium potatoes, peeled and diced
- ❖ 1 clove garlic, halved
- ❖ 4 cups vegetable broth, low sodium preferred
- ❖ 1/4 teaspoon (or about 2 turns of the grinder) freshly cracked black pepper
- ❖ 2 tablespoons extra virgin olive oil

Instructions:

- ❖ Prick the sausages with the tip of a knife then brown them in a saucepan or a griddle with little oil if needed over medium heat. When they are cooked through, slice them.
- ❖ In the slow cooker, put the sausages, potatoes, kale, broth, garlic and pepper.
- ❖ Cover and cook on low 4-5 hours or high 2 to 3 hours. After it is cooked, discard the garlic.
- ❖ Drizzle with extra virgin olive oil before serving.

SNACK RECIPES

Clean-Eating Deviled Eggs

It's everyone's favorite appetizer, snack, and brunch food. The Deviled Egg. Take a hard-boiled egg, shell it, slice it, and fill the yoke with a delicious mix of fresh mayo, spices, and a touch of mustard. Wait. Mayonnaise? Most mayonnaise brands, especially the commercially made varieties, are not on my list of healthy foods, for some reasons.

A Sprinkle some paprika on your eggs to finish, and no one will know the difference between these healthy deviled eggs and the traditional version. But when you tell them to take the second egg, without the guilt, they'll be asking for the recipe!

Yields: 4 servings, Serving Size: 2 deviled eggs, Calories: 115, Total Fat: 6g, Saturated Fat: 1g, Trans Fat: 0g, Cholesterol: 3mg, Sodium: 130mg, Carbohydrates: 13g, Fiber: 1g, Sugars: 1g, Protein: 2g, Smart Points: 5

Ingredients:

- ❖ 4 large eggs, hard-boiled and shells removed
- ❖ 2 tablespoons clean mayo brand
- ❖ 1/2 teaspoon apple cider vinegar

- ❖ 1/2 teaspoon yellow mustard, no sugar added
- ❖ 1/8 teaspoon black pepper
- ❖ 1/4 teaspoon sea salt
- ❖ 1/2 teaspoon paprika for garnish

Instructions:

- ❖ Slice hard boiled eggs in half lengthwise. Remove yolks, add to a small mixing bowl and mash with a fork. Add the remaining ingredients, except paprika, and stir until creamy.
- ❖ Evenly divide mixture inside the cooked egg whites. Sprinkle with paprika and refrigerate until ready to serve.

No-Bake Mini Apple Cheesecakes

So, you've returned from your apple-picking excursion with a bundle of fruit, but aren't quite confident in your baking skills? This no-bake recipe will have you turning out dessert in no time. These mini apple cheesecakes are delicious, and their presentation is so gorgeous that you'll want to invite guests over just to have a chance to serve  them. Plus, with all clean eating ingredients, these mini portions of sweet indulgence are guilt-free.

Yields: 8 servings, Serving Size: 1 ramekin, Calories: 165, Total Fat: 6 g, Saturated Fat: 1 g, Trans Fat: 0 g, Cholesterol: 3 mg, Sodium: 24 mg, Carbohydrates: 26 g, Dietary Fiber: 4 g, Sugars: 20 g, Protein: 5 g, Smart Points: 7

Ingredients:

- ❖ 2 large apples, peeled, cored, and diced (recommend Golden Delicious or Braeburn)
- ❖ 1/4 teaspoon cinnamon
- ❖ 3 tablespoons (Blonde) Coconut Sugar
- ❖ Pinch of sea salt
- ❖ 2/3 cup fat-free cream cheese, softened
- ❖ 1/3 cup fat-free (plain) Greek yogurt
- ❖ 4 dates, no sugar added
- ❖ 1/2 cup walnut halves (about 18)
- ❖ 8 Mini Dessert Dishes, 3 - 4 ounces each

Instructions:

- ❖ Add diced apples, 1 teaspoon coconut sugar, salt, and cinnamon to a medium pot, cover, and cook over medium heat just until apples begin to boil. Reduce heat to a simmer and cook until tender, approximately 30 minutes. Be careful not to turn into applesauce. Allow cooling to room temperature before adding to dessert dishes.
- ❖ While apples are cooking, in a medium mixing bowl add softened cream cheese, yogurt, and remaining coconut sugar. Beat with an electric mixer until smooth and sugar are dissolved, about 2 minutes. Refrigerate until ready to use.
- ❖ Add dates to a food processor and pulse until finely diced. Add walnuts and continue to pulse just until a coarse crumb consistency and combined with dates.
- ❖ Evenly layer to each dessert dish, walnut mixture, cream cheese, and lastly cooked apples. Sprinkle any remaining pecan mixture over the top.
- ❖ Refrigerate until ready to serve.

No-Bake Workout Bars

After a workout, your bodies need to replenish. You need hydrate, and then to choose a healthy snack to balance my electrolytes, allow your muscles to repair themselves with lean protein, and add some superfoods to make sure your body is fueled and working at its optimum level.

Consuming the perfect workout snack within an hour of finishing your workout ensures that the protein and nutrients you consume are utilized efficiently.

It's important to remember that, along with fitness routines that have your hearts racing and our muscles pumping, you need to add meals and snacks to your diet that compliment your workouts and make sure you get the most of each lunge, squat, and minute on the elliptical.

Yields: 12 bars, Serving size: 1 bar, Calories: 333, Total Fat: 18 g, Saturated Fats: 6 g, Trans Fats: 0 g, Cholesterol: 1 mg, Sodium: 14 mg, Carbohydrates: 37 g, Dietary fiber: 5 g, Sugars: 19 g, Protein: 14 g, Smart Points: 13

Ingredients:

- ❖ 2 cups rolled oats
- ❖ 1/2 cup protein powder
- ❖ 1/2 cup mini chocolate chips
- ❖ 1/2 cup chia seeds or ground flax seeds
- ❖ 1/2 cup raisins
- ❖ 1 cup natural peanut butter

- ❖ 1/2 cup lite coconut milk, (more or less as needed to reach desired consistency)
- ❖ 1/4 cup honey (raw honey if possible)

Instructions:

In a blender, pulse 1 1/2 cups of the oats until a flour-like consistency. In a large bowl, toss to combine oat flour, remaining 1/2 cup oats, protein powder, chocolate chips, chia or flax seeds, and raisins.

Stir together in a medium bowl the coconut milk, peanut butter, and honey. Pour peanut butter mixture over oat mixture and stir until thoroughly incorporated.

Spread mixture into a 9 x 9-Inch square pan or an 11 x 7-inch pan. Press mixture down and cover with a lid or foil and refrigerate overnight, or until they harden some. Slice into 12 bars and keep stored in the refrigerator.

Skinny Bell Pepper Chips

Need a little healthy crunch in your life? Try my Skinny Bell Pepper Chips! They are a cinch to make, and so much healthier for you than corn or potato chips. With just a few ingredients and some oven time, you can get that same satisfying crunch without all the fat and calories.

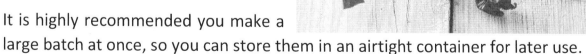

It is highly recommended you make a large batch at once, so you can store them in an airtight container for later use.

Yields: 4 servings, Serving Size: 1/2 bell pepper, Calories: 49, Total Fat: 2g, Saturated Fat: 2g, Trans Fat: 0g, Cholesterol: 0mg, Sodium: 152mg, Carbohydrates: 7g, Fiber: 1g, Sugar: 5g, Protein: 1g, Smart Points: 3

Ingredients:

- ❖ 2 medium red bell peppers, remove seeds, membrane, and core
- ❖ 2 teaspoons honey
- ❖ 2 teaspoons coconut oil
- ❖ 1/4 teaspoon black pepper
- ❖ 1/2 teaspoon kosher or sea salt

Instructions:

- ❖ Slice peppers into 1/4-inch strips and combine with honey, coconut oil, and salt.

Dehydrator Instructions:

- ❖ Place bell pepper strips on dehydrator shelves, ensuring they aren't touching. Turn dehydrator to 125 F, and dehydrate 24 hours or until crispy and able to snap in half. Allow chips to cool completely before storing in an airtight container.

Oven Instructions:

- ❖ Preheat oven to 150 degrees. Place pepper strips on a large nonstick or parchment lined baking sheet, ensure they aren't touching. Place baking sheet on the middle oven rack, leave the oven door slightly ajar, dehydrate until crispy and able to snap in half, about 8 -10 hours. Allow cooling completely before storing in an airtight container.

3-Ingredient Coconut Mango Ice Cream

Looking for a refreshing, healthy way to cool off this summer? Believe it or not, you don't have to dive into a tub of sweet, store-bought ice cream! Make your own creamy, soft-serve style ice cream using just three ingredients: coconut milk, frozen fruit, and honey.

Yields: 6 servings, Serving Size: 1/2 cup, Calories: 193, Total Fat: 9 g, Saturated Fat: 7 g, Trans Fat: 0 g, Cholesterol: 0 mg, Sodium: 9 mg, Carbohydrates: 31 g, Dietary Fiber: 3 g, Sugars: 27 g, Protein: 2 g, Smart Points: 11

Ingredients:

- ❖ ICE CREAM:
- ❖ 1 cup canned Coconut Milk (full fat recommended)
- ❖ 3 cups organic diced mango, frozen
- ❖ 3 tablespoons honey(optional)
- ❖ RASPBERRY SAUCE:
- ❖ 1/3 cup raspberries
- ❖ 3 tablespoons honey, optional pure maple syrup
- ❖ 1 teaspoon chia
- ❖

Instructions:

- ❖ In a hi-speed blender or large food processor, blend coconut milk, frozen mango, and honey until the texture of soft-serve ice cream. Scoop ice cream into serving dishes. Optional Sauce: Puree ingredients for the raspberry sauce in a small food processor. Tip: If using a hi-speed blender, use the tamper that comes with it for a creamier consistency.

Baked Asparagus Fries With Creamy Chipotle Dip

Everyone craves fries now and then. There are few better things than biting into a crisp, hot, and salty fry. Are you salivating yet? Good! Because I have the perfect healthy alternative to your regular fatty fast food fry: my Baked Asparagus Fries with Creamy Chipotle Dip. These asparagus fries have all the crunchy deliciousness of a

potato chip, but they are baked to avoid those pesky empty calories that come from cooking oil. My chipotle dip uses Greek yogurt to achieve the same texture as many milk and egg based dips without loading up on the fat and sugar.

You can whip up a batch in just 20 minutes, so grab some asparagus and enjoy a batch of my baked asparagus fries without guilt.

Yields: 4 servings, Calories: 156, Total Fat: 6g, Saturated Fat: 1g, Trans Fat: 0g, Cholesterol: 15g, Sodium: 246mg, Carbohydrates: 15g, Fiber: 3g, Sugar: 6g, Protein: 12g, Smart Points: 5

Ingredients:

Baked Asparagus Fries

- ❖ 1 pound asparagus spears
- ❖ 1/3 cup whole grain breadcrumbs, optional Panko
- ❖ 1/4 cup finely grated parmesan cheese

- ❖ 1/4 teaspoon black pepper
- ❖ Kosher or sea salt to taste
- ❖ 1/8 teaspoon garlic powder
- ❖ 1/8 teaspoon cayenne pepper
- ❖ 3 tablespoons low-fat milk

Creamy Chipotle Dip

- ❖ 1 cup Greek yogurt
- ❖ 1 tablespoon pureed chipotle peppers (more or less depending on the spice level desired)
- ❖ 1 small garlic clove, crushed and minced
- ❖ Kosher or sea salt

Instructions:

- ❖ Preheat oven to 425 degrees F.
- ❖ Trim ends of asparagus spears.
- ❖ In a small mixing bowl combine bread crumbs, parmesan cheese, black pepper, salt, garlic powder, and cayenne pepper. Dip asparagus into milk and dredge in bread crumbs to coat all sides. Note: It may be necessary to press crumbs onto asparagus to ensure the crumbs stick.
- ❖ Lightly mist a non-stick cookie sheet with cooking spray. And arrange asparagus spears on a cookie sheet, so the spears are not touching. Bake 10-12 minutes or until golden.
- ❖ Creamy Chipotle Dip
- ❖ Combine ingredients in a small bowl and refrigerate until ready to use.

Oven Baked Zucchini Chips

Yields: 4 servings, Calories: 99, Total Fat: 3 g, Saturated Fat: 2 g, Trans Fat: 0 g, Cholesterol: 13, Carbohydrates: 12 g, Sodium: 241 mg, Dietary Fiber: 2 g, Sugars: 2 g, Protein: 6 g, SmartPoints: 3

Ingredients:

- ❖ 1 (large) zucchini, cut into 1/8" - 1/4" slices
- ❖ 1/3 cup whole grain breadcrumbs, optional Panko (homemade breadcrumb recipe)
- ❖ 1/8 teaspoon garlic powder
- ❖ 1/4 cup finely grated parmesan cheese, reduced fat
- ❖ 1/4 teaspoon black pepper
- ❖ Kosher or sea salt to taste
- ❖ 1/8 teaspoon cayenne pepper
- ❖ 3 tablespoons low-fat milk

Instructions:

- ❖ Preheat oven to 425 degrees.
- ❖ Combine in a small mixing bowl, breadcrumbs, parmesan cheese, black pepper, salt, garlic powder, and cayenne pepper. Dip zucchini slices into milk and dredge into bread crumbs to coat both sides. Note: It may be necessary to press crumbs onto zucchini slices to ensure the crumbs stick.
- ❖ Arrange zucchini on a non-stick cookie sheet and lightly mist with a non-stick cooking spray.
- ❖ If using a rack, place rack on a cookie sheet. Bake 15 minutes, turn over and continue baking until golden, approximately 10-15 minutes (being careful not

to burn). Allow cooling to room temperature before storing in an airtight container.

- ❖ TIP: Zucchini Chips will continue to get crispier while cooling.
- ❖ NOTE: For gluten free chips, use gluten-free bread crumbs.

Mini – Banana Pudding

Who doesn't love banana pudding? Now you can enjoy this comfort-food dessert at only 102 calories per serving. This Mini Dessert is perfectly portioned so that you can enjoy this ultra-rich treat without giving a second thought to blowing your healthy eating plan.

Yields: 6, Serving Size: 3.2 ounces, Calories: 102, Total Fat: 2 g, Saturated Fat: 1 g, Trans Fat: 0 g, Cholesterol: 37, Carbohydrates: 19 g, Sodium: 24 mg, Dietary Fiber: 1 g, Sugars: 14 g, Protein: 2 g, SmartPoints: 5

Ingredients:

- ❖ 10 whole almonds
- ❖ 2 tablespoons cornstarch
- ❖ Dash of Kosher or sea salt
- ❖ 3 tablespoons coconut palm sugar
- ❖ 1 egg yolk, slightly beaten
- ❖ 3/4 cup milk, 1 or 2% is recommended, (optional canned lite coconut milk)
- ❖ 1/2 teaspoon vanilla
- ❖ 2 bananas, thinly sliced
- ❖ 6 (4 ounces) dessert dishes

Instructions:

- ❖ Preheat oven to 325 degrees f. Roast almonds 12 minutes and allow to cool while preparing pudding. After cooled, mince almonds in a food processor or use a knife.
- ❖ In a saucepan, combine cornstarch, salt, and sugar. Add egg yolk to dry ingredients. Gradually stir in milk and continue stirring until well combined. Turn to medium heat and cook while stirring constantly. Continue cooking until a pudding-like consistency.
- ❖ Remove from heat, stir in vanilla. While still warm, alternate pudding with bananas in dessert dishes. Sprinkle minced almonds on top of pudding. Top with whipped topping if desired.

Mini Strawberry Cheesecake

Mini Desserts are perfectly portioned for those must have times when a decadent treat is called for. My Mini Cheesecake is the first in a long line of amazingly delicious mini desserts. Now it is true, you can have your cake and eat it too, and no guilt involved.

Mini Desserts are all low-calorie, and all meant to satisfy. These mini desserts are all served in 3-4 ounce dishes.

NOTE: This dessert is low in Saturated Fat, and very low in Cholesterol. It is also an excellent source of Vitamin C.

Yields: 8 servings, Serving Size: 1 (3.2 oz) dish, Calories:138, Total Fat: 2 g, Saturated Fat: 0 g, Trans Fat: 0 g, Cholesterol: 3, Carbohydrates: 27 g, Sodium: 110 mg, Dietary Fiber: 3 g, Sugars: 22 g, Protein: 4 g, SmartPoints: 6

Ingredients:

- ❖ 1/2 cup fat-free cream cheese
- ❖ 2 tablespoons Coconut Palm Sugar
- ❖ 1/2 cup low-fat Greek yogurt
- ❖ 2 teaspoons freshly squeezed lemon juice
- ❖ 1/4 cup strawberry preserves, no sugar added (I used Polaner All Fruit)
- ❖ 1 cup diced strawberries
- ❖ 1/3 cup whole almonds
- ❖ 4 dates, no sugar added
- ❖ 8 Mini Dessert Dishes, 3-4 ounces

Instructions:

- ❖ In a medium mixing bowl, add cream cheese, sugar, yogurt and lemon juice, beat with an electric mixer until smooth and sugar are dissolved, about 3 minutes. Refrigerate until ready to use.
- ❖ In a small bowl, combine preserves and strawberries.
- ❖ Add almonds to a food processor and pulse until a crumb consistency, being careful not to turn into flour. Add dates and pulse until combined.
- ❖ Evenly divide 1/2 almond and date mixture among the dessert dishes. Top with 1/2 cheesecake & yogurt batter, spoon in 1/2 strawberry mixture, add one additional layer of each. Refrigerate 2 -3 hours before serving.
- ❖ These desserts are perfect for preparing ahead of time and enjoying one a day to satisfy that sweet craving. This mini dessert can be placed in a freezer safe dish for enjoying at a later date.

Bell Pepper Nacho Boats

Sure- nachos taste delicious, but they probably don't rank high on the list of nutritious, wholesome recipes, especially when you're trying to eat healthily! However, you can satisfy your cravings for this classic Tex-Mex snack without worrying about your waistline by subbing in bell peppers for regular tortilla chips. This recipe for Bell Pepper Nacho  Boats calls for delicious ingredients, like lean ground meat, savory spices, delicious salsa, and melted cheddar cheese.

Instead of slathering the mixture over carb-laden chips, only stuff the wholesome combination of flavors and textures into nutrient-rich pepper boats. So, eat up!

Yields: 18 boats, Serving: 2 boats, Calories: 145, Total Fat: 9g, Saturated Fat: 4g, Trans Fat: 0g, Cholesterol: 50mg, Sodium: 293mg, Carbohydrates: 4g, Fiber: 1g, Sugars: 2g, Protein: 13g, SmartPoints: 4

Ingredients:

- ❖ 1 pound lean ground turkey
- ❖ 1 teaspoons chili powder
- ❖ 1 teaspoon cumin
- ❖ 1/2 teaspoon black pepper
- ❖ 1/4 teaspoon kosher or sea salt
- ❖ 3/4 cup salsa, no sugar added
- ❖ 1 cup grated cheddar cheese, reduced-fat
- ❖ 3 bell peppers

Instructions:

- ❖ Remove seeds, core, and membrane from bell peppers then slice each one into 6 verticle pieces where they dip down. Set sliced bell peppers aside.
- ❖ Cook ground turkey over medium-high heat, breaking up as it cooks. Cook until the turkey loses its pink color and is cooked through. Drain off any fat.
- ❖ Preheat oven to 375 degrees.
- ❖ Combine cooked turkey with spices and salsa. Evenly distribute mixture into the bell pepper boats, top with cheese. Bake on a parchment lined baking sheet for 10 minutes or until cheese is melted and peppers are hot.
- ❖ NOTE: If you prefer much softer bell peppers, add a few tablespoons water to the bottom of a large casserole dish, add filled nachos, cover tightly with foil and bake 15 minutes.
- ❖ Remove from the oven and add additional toppings, If desired.
- ❖ Optional ingredients: sliced Jalapeno peppers, diced avocado, fat-free Greek yogurt or sour cream, or sliced green onions.

Peanut Butter-Yogurt Dip

You know the feeling. Maybe boredom has set in at work. Maybe stress is affecting you at the end of the day. Or perhaps you're just plain hungry, and only something sweet and creamy will do.

Don't give in to sugary, fattening snacks. Instead, whip up the easiest treat

you'll ever make. My Peanut Butter Yogurt Dip has all of the sweet, nutty, peanut buttery goodness you're craving, with a dose of clean eating Greek yogurt for delicious, creamy texture.

Looking for a way to enjoy your yogurt dip that increases the sweetness, without packing on calories? Try dipping fruit into it for a treat that will satisfy those afternoon cravings or post-dinner munchies. Serve it to kids for a family-friendly snack that is as healthy as it is tasty.

Serving size: 2 tablespoons, Calories: 40, Saturated Fats: 1 gm, Trans Fats: 0 gm, Cholesterol: 0 mg, Sodium: 6 mg, Carbohydrates: 2 gm, Dietary fiber: 0 gm, Sugars: 1 gm, Protein: 2 gm, SmartPoint: 2

Ingredients:

- ❖ 1/2 cup Greek yogurt, fat-free, plain
- ❖ 1/4 cup natural peanut butter, crunchy recommended

Instructions:

- ❖ Combine all the ingredients in a small bowl, refrigerate until ready to eat.
- ❖ Serve with your favorite fruit or veggie.

Beet Chips With Tzatziki Dipping Sauce

What is it about beets that give them such a bad rap? They are vibrant in color, rich in vitamins and nutrients, and oh so versatile.

The rosemary and garlic in this Beet Chips with Tzatziki Dipping Sauce recipe tone down the earthy taste that is sometimes off-putting with beets, leaving you with a satisfyingly crunchy chip that is perfect dipped in Tzatziki sauce.

You can feel good that you're trying a healthier option than plain old potato chips, and giving the sadly overlooked beet a chance. If you have more Tzatziki sauce than you end up needing, save it for a tasty veggie dip.

Yields: 4 servings, Calories: 170, Total Fat: 13g, Saturated Fat: 1g, Trans Fat: 0g, Cholesterol: 10mg, Sodium: 1148mg, Carbohydrates: 9g, Fiber: 1g, Sugar: 6g, Protein: 6g, SmartPoints:6

Ingredients:

Chips

- ❖ 4 medium red and golden beets (if available)
- ❖ 2 teaspoons Kosher or sea salt to taste
- ❖ 1/4 teaspoon fresh rosemary, chopped
- ❖ 1/8 teaspoon garlic powder
- ❖ 2 tablespoons extra-virgin olive oil

Tzatziki Dip

- ❖ 1/4 cup shredded cucumber
- ❖ 1 cup Greek yogurt
- ❖ 2 cloves garlic, smashed and minced
- ❖ 1 tablespoon dry dill
- ❖ 2 teaspoon extra-virgin olive oil
- ❖ 1/4 teaspoon Kosher or sea salt

Instructions:

- ❖ Preheat oven to 450 degrees F.
- ❖ Peel beets and slice 1/8-inch thick. In a small bowl, combine salt, rosemary and garlic powder.
- ❖ Gently toss beets with the olive oil and salt mixture. Line cooking sheet with parchment paper and lightly mist with nonstick cooking spray. Arrange beets on the sheet, so they are not overlapping or touching.
- ❖ Bake 15 minutes, turn over and continue baking until golden, approximately 10-15 minutes (being careful not to burn). Allow cooling to room temperature and store in an airtight container.

Tzatziki Dip

- ❖ Squeeze as much water from the shredded cucumber as possible. Combine cucumber, Greek yogurt, garlic, dill, olive oil, and salt in a bowl. Stir until combined and refrigerate until ready to serve.

Clean Eating Jalapeño Popper Mac And Cheese

On the hunt for fresh jalapeño poppers? How about clean eating mac and cheese? If you've nearly given up on your hopes of enjoying these two dishes in a healthy way, You'll love this jalapeño popper mac and cheese, made with fresh ingredients to keep the calories down and the flavor delicious. A creamy low-fat cheese sauce and crunchy whole  wheat bread crumbs give it the crunch and flavor you love, but add digestible protein and fiber typically not found in a dish like this. The result is a meal that will satisfy you while helping you stick to your diet.

Yields: 6 servings, Serving Size: 3/4 cup, Calories: 351, Total Fat: 14 g, Saturated Fat: 5 g, Trans Fat: 0 g, Cholesterol: 30 mg, Sodium: 496 mg, Carbohydrates: 34 g, Dietary Fiber: 5 g, Sugars: 6 g, Protein: 22 g, SmartPoints: 11

Ingredients:

- ❖ 3 cups dry whole grain macaroni noodles, cooked according to the package directions
- ❖ 2 tablespoons olive oil
- ❖ 1 small onion, diced
- ❖ 2 jalapeño peppers, seeded and diced
- ❖ 1 clove garlic, minced
- ❖ 1 teaspoon mustard powder, (optional 1 tablespoon prepared mustard)
- ❖ 2 tablespoons flour (I used white whole wheat)

- ❖ 2 cups low-fat milk
- ❖ 2 cups low-fat Colby Jack cheese
- ❖ 4 ounces low-fat cream cheese
- ❖ 1/2 cup whole wheat bread crumbs
- ❖ Salt and pepper, ot taste

Instructions:

- ❖ Preheat oven to 400 degrees F.
- ❖ In a large saucepan, heat the olive oil over medium heat. Add the onions and jalapeños and cook until soft, about 5 minutes. Add the garlic and continue cooking 1 more minute. Stir in the mustard powder and flour and season with salt and pepper. Stir for 1 minute.
- ❖ Add the milk and bring to a boil, whisking constantly. Cook for 1 minute and turn off heat. Stir in 1 1/2 cups of the Colby jack and all of the cream cheese. Add the cooked pasta and stir until well coated. Transfer to a casserole dish.
- ❖ Top with breadcrumbs and remaining cheese and bake for 30-35 minutes until top is browned and cheese is bubbly. Allow standing for 5 minutes before serving.

Clean Eating Chicken Fried Rice

Fried foods are irresistible to your taste buds and your waistline. The next time you're tempted to get fattening fried food to-go, pick up the ingredients yourself and cook my Clean Eating Chicken Fried Rice instead.

The nutty brown rice fills you with fiber and minerals, and my stir-fry mix is a powerhouse of healthy ingredients.

Onions, bell peppers, and scallions unleash the full depth of their flavor while frying. Plus, eggs and chicken provide a healthy dose of protein. This delicious stir-fry will fill the whole family with the nutrients they need for a healthy meal.

Yields: 6 servings, Serving Size: 1/2 cup, Calories: 266, Total Fat: 5g, Saturated Fat: 1g, Trans Fat: 0g, Cholesterol: 88mg, Sodium: 254mg, Carbohydrates: 30g, Fiber: 3g, Sugar: 3g, Protein: 23g, SmartPoints: 6

Ingredients:

For The Rice

- ❖ 1 cup long grain brown rice
- ❖ 2 1/2 cups water
- ❖ 1/4 teaspoon salt

For The Fried Rice

- ❖ 1 tablespoon olive oil
- ❖ 1/2 cup chopped onions
- ❖ 1 cup diced bell pepper, red or green
- ❖ 1 tablespoon finely minced, peeled ginger root

- ❖ 3 tablespoons water
- ❖ 2 boneless, skinless chicken breasts, cut into thin strips
- ❖ 2 eggs, beaten
- ❖ 2-3 tablespoons lite soy sauce, optional Tamari
- ❖ 2 teaspoons sesame oil
- ❖ 1/4 cup chopped scallions or green onions, optional

Instructions:

For the rice:

- ❖ Add rice, salt, and water to a pot, stir once, and bring to a boil over high heat. Reduce heat to low and cover. Allow to cook, untouched, for 40 minutes or until tender and liquid is absorbed. Remove from heat and let stand for 5 minutes, covered.
- ❖ Refrigerate rice until cold, preferably overnight.

To fry the rice:

- ❖ Add olive oil to a large nonstick skillet or wok. Over medium heat add chicken, onions, bell pepper, and ginger and cook for about 4 to 5 minutes, until onions are translucent and chicken is mostly cooked through. Add cooked rice and water and increase heat to medium-high.
- ❖ Push rice to one side and add beaten eggs to the other side, scramble quickly then toss in with the rice mixture. Stir in the soy sauce and sesame oil. Remove from the heat and stir in the scallions, if using. Enjoy!

Clean Eating Vegetable Fritters

My fritters are a cinch to fry. All you have to do is prep your veggies, mix the batter, oil your pan, and cook away! I've included zucchini, bell peppers, and scallion to provide strong vegetable flavoring. To draw out their natural goodness, I've spiced up the recipe with earthy thyme and zesty paprika.

Yields: 4 servings, Serving Size: 2 fritters, Calories: 200, Total Fat: 13g, Saturated Fat: 2g, Trans Fat: 0g, Cholesterol: 93mg, Sodium: 202mg, Carbohydrates: 26g, Fiber: 3g, Sugar: 3g, Protein: 6g, SmartPoints: 6

Ingredients:

- ❖ 2 cups grated zucchini, water squeezed out *see instructions
- ❖ 3/4 cup chopped red bell pepper
- ❖ 3/4 cup sliced scallions, greens, and whites, roots discarded
- ❖ 2 tablespoons fresh thyme leaves, optional 2 teaspoons dried thyme
- ❖ 1/2 cup flour, (white whole-wheat was used in this recipe)
- ❖ 2 large eggs, lightly beaten
- ❖ 1/4 teaspoon kosher or sea salt
- ❖ 1/8 teaspoon black pepper
- ❖ 1/8 teaspoon paprika
- ❖ 3 tablespoons olive oil

Instructions:

- ❖ Shred zucchini and place in a colander or fine-mesh sieve set over a bowl. Sprinkle a small amount of salt over the zucchini and let sit for about 10 minutes. Then press on the zucchini to squeeze out any remaining water into the bowl.
- ❖ Whisk eggs in the bottom of a large bowl. Add the zucchini, bell pepper, scallions, flour, salt, pepper, thyme, and paprika to the bowl, stirring to combine completely. Add one tablespoon of the olive oil to a sauté pan over medium heat, and add in a mound of the mixture, pushing with the spatula to flatten into a round. Repeat with 2 more. 3 should fit in the pan.
- ❖ Cook each fritter for 2 to 3 minutes on one side, and then flip and cook for an additional 2 to 3 minutes on the other side, or until golden brown and cooked through.
- ❖ Serve sprinkled with thyme leaves for garnish, and topped with a dollop of light sour cream or Greek yogurt, if desired.

Grilled Salmon Kebobs

When lovely weather appears, it's time to bust out those grills and bring the cuisine outdoors. What better way to enjoy deliciously cooked food than with these incredible salmon kebobs? Gorgeous, flavorful cubes of food are marinated in a mouthwatering mixture of fresh rosemary, savory spices, and a splash of lemon juice. After cooking, they  flaunt a crisp outside with a smooth, flaky inside. The buttery consistency will please even the pickiest taste buds. Each bite packs a boatload of omega-3s, vitamins, and satisfying protein that'll keep you full and ward off future cravings.

Yields: 4 servings, Calories: 308, Total Fat: 22g, Saturated Fat: 5g, Trans Fat: 0g, Cholesterol: 62mg, Sodium: 401mg, Carbohydrates: 2g, Fiber: 1g, Sugar: 0g, Protein: 24g, SmartPoints: 8

Ingredients:

Salmon

- ❖ 1 pound thick wild salmon, without skin, cut into about 12 cubes

Marinade

- ❖ 2 tablespoons extra virgin olive oil
- ❖ 2 tablespoons fresh squeezed lemon juice
- ❖ 3 tablespoons minced fresh rosemary
- ❖ 1 tablespoon dijon mustard
- ❖ 2 cloves garlic, minced
- ❖ 1/2 teaspoon kosher or sea salt
- ❖ 1/2 teaspoon black pepper

❖ 4 skewers, if using bamboo or wood soak in warm water for 20 to 30 minutes

Instructions:

❖ Whisk together all ingredients for the marinade.
❖ Add salmon and let marinate for about 20 minutes at room temperature.
❖ Thread pieces of salmon on skewers.
❖ Coat grates of a grill or a grill pan or skillet with a light layer of cooking spray.
❖ Set to high.

❖ Once hot, add skewers to grill or pan and cook for 3 minutes or so on each side for 6 to 8 minutes, until the fish is opaque and flakes easily with a fork, basting with any leftover marinade while cooking. Enjoy!

Pan-Fried Salmon With Asparagus & Couscous Salad

My Pan-Fried Salmon with Asparagus & Couscous Salad is savory and ultra-nutritious. The balance of heart-healthy protein, nutritious greens, and superfood grains will fill you up with essential nutrients. Half a fillet of salmon contains 40 grams of protein and hardly any calories. Asparagus is chock-full of a long list of vitamins and  minerals. The veggie is mainly full of Vitamin K, folate, and copper. Couscous is a filling, high-fiber, low-fat starch. As a complex carbohydrate, couscous is just what your body needs to stay full and energized throughout the day.

My recipe is a simple one that requires minimal prep and effort. Just cook couscous, blanch asparagus, and fry salmon for a few minutes. You have a scrumptious, well-balanced meal that looks stunning and tastes heavenly. Serve and savor.

Yields: 4 servings, Calories: 308, Total Fat: 13g, Saturated Fat: 3g, Trans Fat: 0g, Cholesterol: 42mg, Sodium: 439mg, Carbohydrates: 27g, Fiber: 3g, Sugars: 3g, Protein: 20g, SmartPoints:9, 1-3/4 cups couscous salad, 3-4 spears asparagus and 1 salmon fillet

Ingredients:

- ❖ 4 (4 ounces) wild caught salmon fillets
- ❖ 1 tablespoon extra-virgin olive oil
- ❖ 1 bunch asparagus, woody bottom stems removed
- ❖ 1 cup (dry) whole wheat couscous
- ❖ 1 red bell pepper, stemmed, seeded, and chopped
- ❖ 1 yellow or orange bell pepper, stemmed, seeded, and chopped
- ❖ 1/4 cup chopped parsley
- ❖ 2 tablespoons freshly squeezed lemon juice, divided
- ❖ 1 teaspoon kosher or sea salt, divided
- ❖ 1/4 teaspoon black pepper

Instructions:

- ❖ In a pot, bring 2/3 cup water with 1/4 teaspoon salt to a boil. Add couscous. Cover and remove from heat. Let sit for 5 minutes or until other ingredients are complete. Remove lid and fluff with a fork.
- ❖ Bring a small pot of water (about 4- 6 cups water) with 1/4 teaspoon salt to a boil. Blanch asparagus for 3 to 4 minutes in boiling water until bright green and crisp-tender. Remove.
- ❖ Sprinkle salmon with salt and pepper. Place oil in a skillet over medium-high heat.
- ❖ Add fillets, skin-side up. Cook for about 3 - 4 minutes until golden on one side.
- ❖ Flip and cook for 3 to 4 more minutes, until skin is crisp and fish is firm.

- ❖ Toss chopped raw peppers and parsley into couscous along with pepper, remaining 1/4 teaspoon salt, and 1 tablespoon lemon juice.
- ❖ Place asparagus on top of couscous. Sprinkle the asparagus with remaining lemon juice. Top with salmon. Serve and enjoy!

Slow Cooker Herb Crusted Turkey Breast

Craving turkey, but don't want the hassle of cooking the whole bird? Have a go at this fabulous slow cooker Herb Crusted Turkey Breast recipe, and it is the perfect size for several servings. You can enjoy it any night of the week, or prepare it for holiday celebrations. The mixture of savory herbs forms a delightful crust that envelopes the juicy

breast meat. If you would like added moisture and flavor, quarter a large apple and onion and place them inside the cavity of the bird before cooking. After 4 or 5 hours in the slow cooker, the turkey will be tender and ready to eat. It is a delicious, straightforward meal that anyone can make.

Serving Size: 1/6 of the finished recipe, Calories: 233, Total Fat: 3 gm, Saturated Fats: 1 gm, Trans Fats: 0 gm, Cholesterol: 112 mg, Sodium: 119 mg, Carbohydrates: 4 gm, Dietary Fiber: 1 gm, Sugars: 1 gm, Protein: 45 gm, SmartPoints: 3

Ingredients:

- ❖ 2 1/2 lb. turkey breast
- ❖ 1 tbsp. garlic powder
- ❖ 1 tbsp poultry seasoning
- ❖ 1 tsp dried thyme

- ❖ 1/4 tsp. black pepper
- ❖ 1 tbsp. onion powder

Instructions:

- ❖ Mix all the spices together in a small mixing bowl.
- ❖ Place your turkey breast on a plate and cover both sides with spices. It should be completely coated in spice mix.
- ❖ Place in slow cooker (no liquid) and cook as directed. Recommend 5-7-quart slow cooker.
- ❖ Time: 4-5 hours or until it reaches at least 165 degrees F. on a meat thermometer.
- ❖ Temp: Low
- ❖ Yield: About 3 servings. Recommended slow cooker size: 5 quarts

Quinoa Stir-Fry

This stir-fry is as easy to whip up as it is healthy. Easy-prep veggies like broccolini and bok choy offer fiber, vitamins, minerals, and antioxidants, while quinoa boosts this dish's fiber content and adds a hefty dose of protein. And with the combined flavors of garlic and soy sauce, you can enjoy the delicious taste of this healthy, vegetarian meal.

Quinoa Stir-Fry is a one-pot meal that can easily be made ahead. Prepare the quinoa the night before, refrigerate, and the remaining work will take less than 10 minutes. This recipe has 10 grams of protein and complex carbohydrates that provide sustainable energy. This dish is good for dinner, lunch, or as a pre-workout food. This recipe is low-calorie with less 300 calories per serving and has little Weight Watchers Points.

Yields: 6 servings, Serving Size: 1 cup, Calories: 269, Total Fat: 10 g, Saturated Fat: 1 g, Trans Fat: 0 g, Cholesterol: 0 mg, Sodium: 134 mg, Carbohydrates: 37 g, Dietary Fiber: 7 g, Sugars: 2 g, Protein: 10 g, SmartPoints: 8

Ingredients:

- ❖ 1 tablespoon extra-virgin olive oil
- ❖ 2 teaspoons sesame seed oil
- ❖ 2 cloves garlic, minced
- ❖ 4 stalks Bok Choy, leaves removed, sliced into 1/2-inch pieces
- ❖ 6 Broccolini or 1 cup broccoli florets
- ❖ 2 tablespoons (low-sodium) soy sauce, more to taste (optional, Tamari)
- ❖ 4 cups cooked and chilled white quinoa (cook according to package instructions)
- ❖ 1/4 cup toasted sesame seed

Instructions:

- ❖ In a large skillet add oils, turn to medium-low heat, sauté garlic until fragrant, about one minute. Add Bok Choy and Broccoli, cover and continue cooking approximately 5 minutes, or until slightly tender.
- ❖ Remove broccolini and set aside.
- ❖ Add soy sauce and cooked quinoa. Stir and cook just until quinoa is heated through. Turn off heat, place broccolini on top of quinoa, sprinkle with toasted sesame seeds. Cover and let rest 5 minutes. Serve immediately.

Easy One-Pot Chicken & Rice Dinner

Combining your ingredients in one large saucepan is a wonderful way to allow flavors to mingle! This Asian dish relies on soy sauce as an essential component. I used freshly-squeezed lemon to balance out the salty flavor. Adding fresh cherry tomatoes, baby corn, and chives give this skillet dinner natural color and taste. The whole family will enjoy this home-cooked, healthy Asian meal.

Yields: 6 servings, Serving Size: 3/4 cup, Calories: 383, Previous Points: 9, Points Plus: 10, Total Fat: 14 g, Saturated Fat: 2 g, Trans Fat: 0 g, Cholesterol: 48 mg, Sodium: 355 mg, Carbohydrates: 42 g, Dietary Fiber: 1 g, Sugars: 2 g, Protein: 21 g

Ingredients:

- ❖ 1 1/2 cups dry basmati or brown rice
- ❖ 2 3/4 cups water
- ❖ 1/4 cup lite (low-sodium) soy sauce, optional Tamari
- ❖ 1/2 cup lemon juice (from 1 lemon)
- ❖ 5 tablespoons extra-virgin olive oil
- ❖ 1 pound chicken white meat, strips
- ❖ 8 pieces baby corn or 1/2 cup regular corn kernels
- ❖ 1/2 teaspoon salt
- ❖ 1/4 teaspoon ground pepper
- ❖ 1 cup cherry tomatoes, halved
- ❖ 2 tablespoons chives, finely chopped

Instructions:

- ❖ Over high heat, in a medium cooking pot, mix the rice and 2-1/2 cups of water then let it boil. When it boils, put down the heat to the lowest, cover partially (leave about a 1/2 inch of opening) and simmer until the rice is cooked through. Note: if you can cook the rice hours ahead, it's better.
- ❖ In a small bowl, mix the soy sauce, lemon and the remaining 1/4 cup of water. Adjust the taste if needed then set aside. Over medium heat, in a large saucepan with 2 tablespoons extra virgin olive oil, sautè the chicken until cooked through. Pour the soy-lemon mixture and add the baby corn then simmer for 15 minutes.
- ❖ Separate the sauce, the corn, and the chicken in three bowls. Still, in the same saucepan, pour the 2 tablespoons of extra virgin olive oil. When the oil is hot, add the chicken until golden brown. Season with the 1/4 teaspoon salt and pepper. Again, take them away from the saucepan and put them in a bowl. In the same pan, pour the remaining extra virgin olive oil, then add the soy-lemon mixture and cook for 3 - 5 minutes or until it thickens slightly. Add the rice and mix well until the rice becomes brown. Move the rice to one side of the saucepan.
- ❖ Put the chicken to the other side of the saucepan and the baby corn on top. Turn off the heat.
- ❖ Put the tomatoes in one corner of the saucepan. Sprinkle with the remaining salt. Sprinkle the chives.

Grilled Turkey Burgers with Cucumber Salad

What's more satisfying than biting into a juicy, flavorful turkey burger? When trying to live a healthy lifestyle, burgers might be out of the picture. However, subbing lean ground turkey in for conventional meat slashes that mega-calorie tally and delivers a great dose of satisfying protein. This grilled turkey burger recipe calls for fresh ingredients like chopped parsley, crunchy onions, and garlic. These grilled turkey burgers are packed with nutrients and offer that rich, meaty flavor you crave without upping your cholesterol levels.

I've paired my recipe with a lovely cucumber salad. Bright, refreshing cucumbers and tomatoes are dressed with chives and coated with a splash of lime juice. The garden-fresh side forms a perfect flavor combo with the turkey burgers.

Yields: 4 servings, Serving Size: 1 patty and 1/4 cup salad, Calories: 314, Total Fat: 17g, Saturated Fat: 4g, Trans Fat: 0g, Cholesterol: 130mg, Sodium: 637mg, Carbohydrates: 15g, Fiber: 2g, Sugar: 3g, Protein: 26g, SmartPoints: 8

Ingredients:

Turkey burgers

- ❖ 1 pound lean ground turkey
- ❖ 1 large egg, beaten
- ❖ 1/2 cup plain whole wheat bread crumbs or whole wheat panko
- ❖ 1/3 cup grated or finely chopped onions
- ❖ 1/3 cup finely chopped parsley
- ❖ 1 clove garlic, minced
- ❖ 1/2 teaspoon kosher or sea salt
- ❖ 1/2 teaspoon black pepper

- ❖ 1 tablespoon extra-virgin olive oil
- ❖ 2 teaspoons canola oil or cooking spray to lightly coat the pan or grill

Cucumber salad

- ❖ 1 cucumber, diced small
- ❖ 1/2 cup chopped chives or green onions
- ❖ 1 medium-sized ripe tomato, finely diced
- ❖ 2 tablespoons freshly squeezed lime or lemon juice
- ❖ 1/4 teaspoon kosher or sea salt

Instructions:

- ❖ Combine all ingredients for turkey burgers, except olive oil.
- ❖ Form into 4 to 5 patties.
- ❖ Sprinkle each patty on both sides with olive oil, using fingers to coat. Lightly oil grates of the grill.
- ❖ Set grill to medium-high heat or place a lightly-oiled skillet or grill pan on the stovetop over medium-high heat.
- ❖ Add patties to grill or skillet and cover (cover if using the grill) and grill for 5 to 6 minutes on each side, until cooked through.
- ❖ Meanwhile, mix all ingredients for cucumber salad. Serve room temperature or chill until serving.

Tangerine Grilled Tuna

Yields: 2 servings, Serving Size: 1 tuna steak, Calories: 421, Total Fat: 21.2 g, Saturated Fat: 3.3 g, Trans Fat: 0 g, Cholesterol: 28 mg, Sodium: mg, Carbohydrates: 39.5 g, Dietary Fiber: 10.9 g, Sugars: 23.5 g, Protein: 24.1 g, SmartPoints: 14

Ingredients:

- ❖ 2 Tuna steaks
- ❖ Watercress
- ❖ 10 Cherry tomatoes halved
- ❖ 1 tsp olive oil (for drizzle)

For marinade:

- ❖ 2 oz tangerine juice
- ❖ 2 tsp sea salt
- ❖ 1 tsp ground black peppercorn
- ❖ 1 tsp ground ginger
- ❖ For Tangerine Carrot Dressing
- ❖ 2 tbsp olive oil
- ❖ 1 tsp ground ginger
- ❖ 1 tsp roasted garlic
- ❖ 4 oz chopped red onions
- ❖ 1 cup baby carrots
- ❖ Juice of 1 tangerine
- ❖ Salt and pepper to taste

Instructions:

- ❖ Rinse tuna steaks under cold running water and set in a deep dish
- ❖ In another mixing bowl, combine all ingredients for marinade and pour over tuna. Set in refrigerator for 1 hour
- ❖ Place all ingredients for dressing in a food processor or blender and puree. That will yield about 9 oz of the dressing.
- ❖ Take 2 tbsp of dressing and place in a mixing bowl. Place watercress and cherry tomatoes in the bowl and toss, coating well with dressing. Place in refrigerator to chill
- ❖ Heat grill and spray with Pam grilling spray.
- ❖ Lightly drizzle olive oil on tuna and place oiled side down on the grill. Oil the upper side as well.
- ❖ Grill for 6 minutes, then flips and cook for 6 minutes on the other side. Your steak should be cooked medium well using this time frame. If you prefer a rarer Tuna steak, cut the time down to 4 minutes on each side.
- ❖ Tuna tends to be dry so be careful not to overcook, and you will have soft, moist and tasty results!
- ❖ To plate, place salad in the middle of the platter and place tuna atop the salad. Enjoy!

Slow Cooker Indian Chicken And Rice

Your family and friends will be impressed with this aromatic and flavorful Biryani-inspired dish.

Slow Cooker Indian Chicken and Rice is a great alternative to carrying out and includes healthy whole grains and protein. Best of all, your leftovers can be heated the next day for a hearty lunch.

Slow cooker recipes are a great option for busy families on the go or just for those who prefer to spend their time doing something other than slaving away in the kitchen.

Serving Size: 3/4 cup, Calories: 254, Total Fat: 4, Saturated Fat: 1 g, Trans Fat: 0 g, Cholesterol: 24 mg, Sodium: 307 mg, Carbohydrates: 34 g, Sugars: 3 g, Dietary Fiber: 3 g, Protein: 18 g, SmartPoints: 7

Ingredients:

- ❖ 3 chicken breasts (2 lbs), skinless, boneless, cut into 1" strips
- ❖ 1 cup long grain brown rice (uncooked)
- ❖ 1/2 cup Greek Yogurt, low fat, plain
- ❖ 2 cups chicken broth, fat-free, low-sodium
- ❖ 1 (4 oz.) can Green Chile Peppers, drained and diced
- ❖ 1/4 teaspoon ginger
- ❖ 1/4 teaspoon cinnamon
- ❖ 1/4 teaspoon cloves
- ❖ 1/4 teaspoon turmeric
- ❖ 1/2 teaspoon cayenne pepper
- ❖ 1 teaspoon black pepper

- ❖ 1 teaspoon chili powder
- ❖ 1 teaspoon coriander
- ❖ 1 teaspoon curry
- ❖ 1 teaspoon paprika
- ❖ Salt to taste
- ❖ 1 Bay Leaf
- ❖ 4 tablespoons fresh mint leaves
- ❖ 1 tablespoon Extra Virgin olive oil
- ❖ 1 medium onion, cut into thin rings
- ❖ 2 cloves garlic, minced

Instructions:

- ❖ In a medium skillet add 1 tablespoon Extra Virgin olive oil and sauté onion and garlic on medium heat, cook for about 5 minutes or until onion is tender.
- ❖ Set aside 2 tablespoons mint leaves for garnish and 5-6 sautéed onion rings for garnish.
- ❖ In a large mixing bowl add sautéed onion and garlic, all other spices and herbs, Greek yogurt, chicken broth and chicken strips; stir to coat chicken thoroughly. Cover and place chicken mixture in the refrigerator for 1-2 hours, allowing the flavors time to meld. Turn slow cooker to high.
- ❖ Add rice (uncooked) on the bottom of the slow cooker. Add chicken mixture over rice, cover and cook on high 3-4 hours or low 5-6. Check after 2 hours two hours to see if additional liquid is needed if so, add another 1/2 cup chicken broth. Cook until chicken is cooked through and rice is tender. Remove bay leaf. Garnish with remaining mint leaves and onion rings and a few raisins if desired.

Baked Sweet Potatoes With Crispy Kale And Feta

Sick of the same 'ol same 'ol? Looking for something seriously different to bring to next weekend's party or to help make dinner a bit more interesting again? Well, look no further than this recipe. Roasted Sweet Potatoes with Crispy Kale and Feta recipe! Even the name is probably more exciting than anything else you've eaten this week,

and potentially this month, right? That's what I thought.

It is THE baked sweet potato dish to rock your socks and those of your guests, family, and friends, too. Not only is it super flavorful, but it boasts a veritable feast of nutrients as well. Sweet potato packs a beta-carotene punch with a healthy dose of vitamin C and dietary fiber. Kale also delivers dietary fiber, in addition to calcium and potassium. You're set with these two powerhouse superfoods, guaranteed to add a great helping of nutrition to your day.

Think cooking up sweet potatoes along with Kale, and adding some feta flavor, seems like it might entail too much work? Well, think again. All you need to do to follow this healthy sweet potato recipe is to bake the potatoes, cook the kale, and then pile on the goodness with some feta, and perhaps a few walnuts for flair. It could not be simpler. So, what are you waiting for? Get your Roasted Sweet Potatoes with Crispy Kale and Feta butt in gear. You'll be glad you did.

Yields: 8 servings, Calories: 171, Total Fat: 9 g, Saturated Fat: 3 g, Trans Fat: 0 g, Sodium: 261 mg, Cholesterol: 98 mg, Carbohydrates: 17 g, Fiber: 3 g, Sugars: 4 g, Protein: 16 g, SmartPoints: 6

Ingredients:

- ❖ 4 large sweet potatoes
- ❖ 1 small bunch curly kale, center ribs removed and cut into bite-size pieces
- ❖ 1 tablespoon olive oil
- ❖ 1 teaspoon sea salt
- ❖ 1/2 teaspoon black pepper
- ❖ 1/2 cup walnut pieces
- ❖ 3/4 cup crumbled feta cheese

Instructions:

For the sweet potatoes:

- ❖ Preheat oven to 400 degrees.
- ❖ Scrub potatoes, wipe dry and place on a baking sheet. Bake 45-55 minutes, or until potatoes are tender when pierced with a fork. While potatoes are baking, in a medium skillet, toss the chopped kale in olive oil, salt, and pepper. Over medium heat, sauté kale until slightly wilted, about 5 minutes.

To assemble:

- ❖ Slice sweet potatoes in half lengthwise. Use a fork to loosen potato and add kale, feta, and walnuts. Return to oven for 10 -12 minutes to melt the feta and Enjoy

Chocolate Meal Replacement Shake

Meal replacement bars and shakes can be helpful in a pinch. I've been there. Your layover is only 30 minutes long, so that bar in your carry-on bag is your only source of energy for the day. You've got 15 minutes to pick up the kids from school, and that canned shake in the cabinet will give you the time you need to head out the door.

But have you ever looked at the labels on many meal replacement drinks and bars? Sure, they may contain ingredients that fulfill the most basic of your needs, but they also contain a whole lot of other ingredients, some of which may be additives, preservatives, or pure ingredients that aren't good for you.

Yields: 1 serving, Calories: 245, Total Fat: 8g, Saturated Fat: 2g, Trans Fat: 0g, Cholesterol: 0mg, Sodium: 154mg, Carbohydrates: 44g, Fiber: 7g, Sugars: 27g, Protein: 20g, SmartPoints: 11

Ingredients:

- ❖ 1 cup almond milk, unsweetened
- ❖ 1 frozen banana (pre-sliced)
- ❖ 2 scoops (one serving) Clean chocolate protein powder
- ❖ 1 tablespoon ground flax seed, optional chia seeds

Instructions:

- ❖ Add all ingredients to a blender and pulse until smooth. Add ice if a thicker shake is desired or additional almond milk for a thinner shake.

Banana Split Protein Smoothie

It's no secret that smoothies are one of my favorite ways to start the day. First of all, they're easy. Combine your favorite fruits in a blender, add your choice of nut milk along with some Greek yogurt, and add flavoring components and nutritional additions such as honey or whey protein, and you've got a breakfast in a glass that beats  out most breakfast dishes from a nutritional standpoint, and a taste perspective as well!

Everyone loves a banana split. Especially in summer, that creamy, dreamy, fruity ice cream treat from childhood stays in our heads until we satisfy our craving! I. have devised a healthy smoothie recipe that will ease your need without packing on the extra fat, calories and sugar.

Greek yogurt and almond milk, when chilled and blended, are a creamy substitute for ice cream that loses the fat and calories, but provides a massive dose of lean protein. Almonds and protein powder elevate the protein quotient, and strawberries and bananas contain all of the fiber, potassium, and antioxidants your body needs to get through a busy morning. Simply blend these ingredients together with ice, and you have a treat that can pass for a banana split regarding flavor, but powers your body for hours without packing on the pounds.

So, fire up your blender and get ready for dessert for breakfast! Your brain won't know you're eating clean, but your body will.

Yields: 2 servings, Serving Size: 1 glass, Calories: 217, Total Fat: 4 g, Saturated Fat: 1 g, Trans Fat: 0 g, Cholesterol: 8 mg, Sodium: 150 mg, Carbohydrates: 29 g, Dietary Fiber: 3 g, Sugars: 19 g, Protein: 17 g, SmartPoints: 8

Ingredients:

- ❖ 1/2 cup non-fat Greek yogurt
- ❖ 1/2 cup unsweetened almond milk (can be replaced with other kinds of low-fat milk)
- ❖ 1 tablespoon unsalted almonds
- ❖ 1/2 cup strawberries, hulled and rinsed
- ❖ 1 banana, peeled and sliced
- ❖ 2 scoops protein powder (clean protein powder)
- ❖ Ice

Instructions:

- ❖ Put all the ingredients, except ice in a blender then pulse until smooth.
- ❖ Add the ice then pulse again until smooth. Serve immediately.

Green Smoothie

If you're a green smoothie holdout, this will be the one to win you over. This green smoothie recipe is ultra-creamy, thick and rich with flavor. The fruit overpowers the kale taste, the avocado gives it the creamy texture, and the ginger root makes for a surprising twist. And, by making your smoothie, you know exactly what ingredients are used, and it's all good!

Yields: 2, Serving Size: 1-1/2 cups, Calories: 118, Total Fat:4 g, Saturated Fat:1 g, Trans Fat: 0 g, Sodium: 22 mg, Carbohydrates: 16 g, Fiber: 2, Sugars: 6 g, Protein: 3 g, SmartPoints: 4

Ingredients:

- ❖ 1 frozen banana, pre-sliced
- ❖ 12 red grapes
- ❖ 2 large kale leaves, stem removed
- ❖ 1/2 avocado, peeled
- ❖ 1/2 knuckle ginger root
- ❖ 1/1/2 - 2 cups chilled water, depending on thickness preferred
- ❖ 6 ice cubes

Instructions:

- ❖ Add all ingredients to a blender and pulse until smooth and creamy.

Chocolate Peanut Butter Protein Smoothie

The combination of chocolate and peanut butter makes a smoothie even the youngest member of the family will devour.

Cocoa powder and peanut butter are crowd-pleasers, while banana and Greek yogurt add potassium and protein to this sweet, satisfying, and nutritious smoothie. Calculated with natural peanut butter and coconut palm sugar

Yields: 3 servings, Serving Size: 1 cup, Calories: 214, Total Fat: 11 g, Saturated Fat: 0 g, Trans Fat: 0 g, Cholesterol: 5, Carbohydrates: 22 g, Sodium: 57 mg, Dietary Fiber: 4 g, Sugars: 10 g, Protein: 10 g, SmartPoints: 7

Ingredients:

- ❖ 2 tablespoons cocoa powder
- ❖ 3 tablespoons natural peanut butter (optional, organic powdered peanut butter which is much lower in fat & calories than regular peanut butter.)
- ❖ 1 cup low-fat milk, (optional, almond or soy milk)
- ❖ 1 frozen banana, pre-sliced
- ❖ 1/2 cup plain greek yogurt, fat-free
- ❖ 2 tablespoons coconut palm sugar, honey is optional
- ❖ 1/2 teaspoon pure vanilla extract
- ❖ Ice as needed

Instructions:

- ❖ Combine all ingredients in a blender and blend until smooth. Add ice according to desired thickness.

Wild Blueberry, Mint, And Flax Seed Smoothie

With just five ingredients, all of them whole and nutritious, you'll whip up this sweet and refreshing smoothie in a snap. Blueberries provide antioxidants, fiber, and sweetness, while flax seeds offer omega-3 fatty acids and fiber. Blended with almond milk, this quenching smoothie adds a dose of cooling mint and sweet honey for an inventive treat that you'll  want to sip any time you need a refreshing, energizing drink.

Yields: 2 servings, Serving Size: 1 1/4 cups, Calories: 200, Total Fat: 7 g, Saturated Fat: 3 g, Trans Fat: 0 g, Cholesterol: 18 mg, Sodium: 136 mg, Carbohydrates: 26 g, Dietary Fiber: 2 g, Sugars: 23 g, Protein: 10 g, SmartPoints: 9

Ingredients:

- ❖ 1 tablespoon flax seeds
- ❖ 2 cups chilled almond milk (or dairy milk)
- ❖ 1/4 cup blueberries, fresh or frozen 1 tablespoon honey or another sweetener (if almond milk is unsweetened)
- ❖ 2 fresh mint leaves

Instructions:

- ❖ Add all the ingredients in a blender and pulse until smooth. Serve!

Coconut Milk Smoothie

Get ready to cheer, coconut lovers! This Coconut Milk Smoothie is going to knock your socks off! Not only does it offer all the sweet, creamy flavor that you've come to adore, but it also contains two added superfood ingredients banana and spinach! Plus, at only 134 calories per serving, what's not to love?! It is one of my best smoothie recipes.

A coconut milk smoothie is an excellent option for vegans and those choosing to go dairy-free for other reasons. Coconut milk contains healthy fat and is a good alternative to cow's milk. It also gives your smoothie a creamier texture than almond milk, juice, or water. You'll swear you are enjoying a thick, creamy milkshake, minus all the unhealthy ingredients.

Delicious smoothies are perfect for a liquid breakfast, a mid-morning snack, a post-workout pick-me-up, or a dessert substitution. They taste sweet because they are usually made with fruit, but they are much lower in calories. When you "hide" extra healthy ingredients like the spinach found in this smoothie, it packs an even more powerful health punch. Try experimenting with green food additions in your smoothie to get the greatest benefits. It is also an excellent way to sneak veggies into a child's diet.

Serving Size: 1/2 the recipe, Calories: 134, Total Fat: 8 gm, Saturated Fats: 6 gm, Trans Fats: 0 gm, Cholesterol: 0 mg, Sodium: 77 mg, Carbohydrates: 15 gm, Dietary Fiber: 2 gm, Sugars: 7 gm, Protein: 3 gm, SmartPoints: 6

Ingredients:

- ❖ 1 1/2 cups coconut milk
- ❖ 1 frozen banana
- ❖ 2 cups raw baby spinach

Instructions:

- ❖ Place all ingredients in a blender and blend until smooth. Add ice for a thicker smoothie.

Morning Power-Up Energy Shake

Wake up and feel great by drinking something energizing and full of ingredients that any nutritionist would approve of. This shake contains flax which is incredibly nutritious thanks to the omega-3 fatty acids and fibers. Besides, the bananas provide a heaping dose of potassium along with numerous other vitamins and minerals.

By adding some protein powder, you will be assured to get that essential protein building block. One of the main contributors to this healthy shake is kale, one of the most praised superfoods in the planet. So, pop a straw in this refreshingly yummy, thick, and cold Morning Power-Up Energy Shake!

Yields: 1 serving, Calories: 323, Total Fat: 8 g, Saturated Fat: 1 g, Trans Fat: 0 g, Sodium: 166 mg, Cholesterol: 6 mg, Carbohydrates: 24 g, Fiber: 5 g, Sugars: 10 g, Protein: 20 g, SmartPoints: 9

Ingredients:

- ❖ 1/2 frozen banana
- ❖ 3/4 cup almond milk
- ❖ 1/2 cup chopped kale
- ❖ 1/4 cup non-fat Greek yogurt
- ❖ 1 tablespoon almond butter
- ❖ 1 serving protein powder (we used Clean Protein Powder)
- ❖ 1 tablespoon ground flax seeds

Instructions:

Add all ingredients to a blender and pulse until combined and creamy. Add a few ice cubes if you prefer a thicker shake. Serve immediately.

Super Green Detox Drink

This Super Green Detox Drink is the perfect beverage to whip up after a night of indulging. From the infinite spectrum of green juices to green smoothies, green-based drinks are certainly trending these days, and for a good reason! These nutrient-rich juices nourish and detoxify your system, and help you feel great. This

recipe in particular calls for powerful superfoods like kale, spinach, and cilantro, ingredients that offer countless health benefits your body will thank you for. And if the thought of sipping on liquefied veggies makes you cringe, don't worry! I've added an apple to the recipe for a hint of sweetness that cranks up the flavor.

Yields: 1 servings, Serving Size: 1 smoothie, Calories: 158, Total Fat: 1 g, Saturated Fat: 0 g, Trans Fat: 0 g, Cholesterol: 0 mg, Sodium: 112 mg, Carbohydrates: 39 g, Dietary Fiber: 9 g, Sugars: 20 g, Protein: 5 g, SmartPoints: 7

Ingredients:

- ❖ 2 celery stalks, chopped
- ❖ 1 small cucumber, chopped
- ❖ 2 kale leaves
- ❖ 1 handful spinach
- ❖ Handful of fresh parsley or cilantro
- ❖ 1 lemon peeled
- ❖ 1 apple, seeded, cored and chopped
- ❖ 2 teaspoons chia seeds

Instructions:

- ❖ If using a juicer: Add all the above ingredients, except chia seeds, to a juicer and juice. Stir in chia seeds before drinking.
- ❖ If using a blender: Add all the above ingredients to a blender along with 1 cup chilled water. Add ice if desired. Blend until smooth. If no pulp is desired, strain smoothie through a fine mesh strainer before drinking.

Kale & Orange Smoothie

Slurp up this tasty blend of delicious greens, lush fruits, and wholesome ingredients. My Kale Orange Smoothie contains the perfect serving of powerful superfoods your body needs.

Fresh kale leaves give the beverage its vibrant color and load it with tons of vitamins and minerals. Frozen bananas lend creaminess to the texture, and raw honey gives the smoothie a hint of sweetness.

Yields: 2 servings, Calories: 127, Total Fat: 0g, Saturated Fat: 0g, Trans Fat: 0g, Cholesterol: 0mg, Sodium: 184mg, Carbohydrates: 23g, Fiber: 7g, Sugar: 12g, Protein: 4g, SmartPoints: 5

Ingredients:

- ❖ 1 frozen banana, peeled, chopped
- ❖ 1 cup loosely packed kale leaves
- ❖ 1 whole orange, peeled
- ❖ 2 teaspoons raw honey, optional
- ❖ 2 cups almond milk

Instructions:

- ❖ Add all ingredients to the blender and pulse until smooth. Add ice cubes, if desired. Enjoy!

Superfood Strawberry And Goji Berry Smoothie

Strawberries are delicious in smoothies, and I love to load them into in a blender with other nutritional superfoods like goji berries and almond milk, or any healthy low-fat milk of your choice. I sweeten this smoothie with a touch of honey. Feel free to use other unrefined sweeteners like maple syrup or stevia. Take a break from your  usual morning smoothie and enjoy this healthy and delicious superfood drink.

Yields: 2 servings, Serving Size: 1 cup, Calories: 197, Total Fat: 5 g, Saturated Fat: 3 g, Trans Fat: 0 g, Cholesterol: 18 mg, Sodium: 147 mg, Carbohydrates: 30 g, Dietary Fiber: 2 g, Sugars: 21 g, Protein: 3 g, SmartPoints: 9

Ingredients:

- ❖ 2 tablespoons dried goji berries
- ❖ 1 cup strawberries, hulled
- ❖ 2 teaspoons honey, optional
- ❖ 2 cups almond milk (optional, low-fat milk)
- ❖ Ice

Instructions:

- ❖ In a small bowl mix the goji berries and 1 tablespoon of water, allow setting for 15 minutes to make the berries softer. In a blender, add the goji berries, strawberries, honey, almond milk and ice and blend until smooth. Serve and enjoy!

Spinach And Mango Smoothie

Sometimes just three simple ingredients combine to bring you a smoothie offering more health benefits than many people enjoy in an entire day. Mango, spinach, and coconut milk or almond milk, when combined, provide you with vitamins, minerals, antioxidants, and fiber in levels you just can't achieve without a powerhouse of a superfood smoothie.

Mangoes are loaded with ingredients that do amazing things for your body. They contain a multitude of cancer-fighting antioxidants and fight cholesterol with their high fiber and pectin levels. Mango helps to regulate insulin levels and is an excellent food for preventing pre-diabetes, as it has a low glycemic index. Its high levels of vitamin C boost the immune system, and its abundance of vitamin A improve eyesight. Plus, mangoes are rich in iron, making them an excellent way to load up on this essential mineral, even if you're staying away from meat.

And of course, spinach is one of my favorite, and most versatile, superfoods. You'll barely notice that it's present in this mango-flavored smoothie, but its health benefits are undeniable. Filled with iron, that precious mineral that's hard to come by when eating a vegetarian diet, and packed with fiber, this leafy green has it all. Phytonutrients and antioxidants make spinach heart healthy, a cancer fighter, and great for the immune system.

Choose a coconut milk or almond milk for a creamy smoothie without added fat and calories. And because this smoothie has only three ingredients, you can whip it up daily with ease.

Calculated with almond milk **Yields:** 1 serving, Serving Size: makes 1-3/4 cups with ice, Calories: 233, Total Fat: 5 g, Saturated Fat: g, Trans Fat: 0 g, Cholesterol: 15 mg, Sodium: 63 mg, Carbohydrates: 15 g, Dietary Fiber: 4 g, Sugars: 38 g, Protein: 10 g, SmartPoints: 11

Ingredients:

- ❖ 1/4 cup almonds
- ❖ 1 cup baby spinach
- ❖ 1 ripe mango, peeled and pitted
- ❖ 3/4 cup unsweetened almond or coconut milk (canned lite variety or from a carton)
- ❖ Ice, if desired
- ❖ Soak 1/2 teaspoon chia seeds in almond milk before adding, if desired
- ❖ Spirulina can be added to this smoothie if desired

Instructions:

- ❖ Blend the almonds until thoroughly ground into a powder. Add all of the rest of the ingredients and mix. Add ice to blender and puree or add it at the end, if desired.

Pumpkin Spice Smoothie

Now, you typically wouldn't have pumpkin pie for breakfast, but with this Pumpkin Spice Smoothie, it's like the best of both worlds! I've taken fresh pumpkin puree and transformed it into a pumpkin smoothie unlike any other.

This good smoothie-banana, fresh pumpkin puree, and lots of fall spices. I've sweetened this drink with pure maple syrup to offset the spice from the nutmeg and cinnamon.

Thick, creamy, and full of just enough fabulous flavor, this smoothie is a filling breakfast that gives you lasting energy that lasts for hours!

Yields: 2 servings, Serving Size: 1 cup, Calories: 138, Total Fat: 2 g, Saturated Fat: 1 g, Trans Fat: 0 g, Cholesterol: 9 mg, Sodium: 69 mg, Carbohydrates: 25 g, Dietary Fiber: 2 g, Sugars: 18 g, Protein: 5 g, SmartPoints: 6

Ingredients:

- ❖ ½ cup [pumpkin puree, fresh or canned
- ❖ 1 frozen banana
- ❖ 1 cup almond milk, optional soy, lite coconut or skim milk
- ❖ 1 tablespoon pure maple syrup, more or less to taste
- ❖ ¼ tsp vanilla
- ❖ ¼ tsp cinnamon
- ❖ 1/8 tsp nutmeg
- ❖ 1/8 tsp allspice
- ❖ ½ cup ice

Instructions:

❖ Puree all ingredients in a blender until smooth.

CONCLUSION

Thanks again for taking the time to buy this book!

You should now have a good understanding of meal prepping, and how to prepare different kinds of recipes.

Thank you!